TOXIC RELATIONSHIPS DECODED - ESCAPE MANIPULATION AND REBUILD YOUR LIFE

Recognize Gaslighting, Narcissism and Other Controlling Behaviors

SELENA MORGAN

Contents

Introduction

Alice and Bob were discussing their weekend plans when Bob suddenly accused Alice of forgetting to book the restaurant, he had asked her to. Alice was confused because she didn't remember Bob ever mentioning the restaurant. When she expressed her confusion, Bob insisted that they had discussed it multiple times and that Alice's forgetting was typical, suggesting she was becoming very forgetful and unreliable. Alice began to question her own memory, feeling distressed and anxious about her apparent forgetfulness, even though she still didn't recall such a conversation.

Later that evening, Alice reviewed her texts and emails to check for any mention of the restaurant reservation. Finding no evidence of the conversation, she approached Bob with this information. Bob laughed it off, saying she probably deleted it because she was too embarrassed to admit her mistake. He remarked that her inability to remember such important things was concerning and maybe she should see a professional. This left Alice feeling even more unsure of her own reality and deeply unsettled by how easily she could supposedly forget such important discussions.

Sound familiar? I too could not escape a toxic relationship. For thirteen long years, my life was a mess of confusion, overshadowed by toxicity. Trapped in a marriage that I eventually came to understand as extremely toxic. At one point I thought to myself, "I feel more secure and confident when he is not around." That moment of realization was like a sudden break in the storm clouds, revealing the possibility of a different, healthier, brighter existence that was within my reach. I want you to know that if I could find my way to the sunlight, so can you. My journey through those shadows is the foundation of this book, and I share it not just as an author, but as a fellow traveler on the path you may be navigating now.

Every year, millions find themselves caught in the web of toxic relationships, struggling for breath under the weight of manipulation and diminished self-worth. If you're reading this, you might seek a beacon of hope, a guide out of the darkness. This book is that guiding light—aiming to illuminate your path away from pain and lead you toward a life of empowerment and fulfillment.

This book harnesses a unique, multidisciplinary approach, blending psychological insights, practical self-help strategies, and real-life stories from survivors across all walks of life. It includes a special focus on the experiences of those in LGBTQIA+ relationships. You'll find interactive elements like reflective journal prompts, and worksheets to engage with and apply what you learn directly to your experiences.

Toxic relationships come in many forms—romantic entanglements, familial bonds, workplace connections, and friendships. This book addresses them all, providing the tools to recognize harmful patterns no matter the context. By educating you on terms like gaslighting, breadcrumbing, and narcissism, we'll build a common language, empowering you to identify and articulate your experiences.

Our primary goal is to equip you with the tools to escape toxic dynamics and pave the way for a deep healing process. This journey is about you, your strength, and your resilience. It's about challenging you to learn how to manage or leave toxic relationships in all their forms, and, most importantly, encouraging you to trust your instincts again. While some themes may naturally reoccur due to the depth and breadth of the topic, I craft each chapter to bring you fresh insights and perspectives, ensuring a continually engaging and enlightening experience.

Think of this book as a trusted companion in your quest for personal growth and self-discovery. Each chapter is a steppingstone, guiding you from understanding and recognizing toxic relationships to escaping them and then on to healing and thriving. It's a journey that will empower you, inspire you, and ultimately, help you rewrite your story.

As we turn the page, remember this is not just about surviving; it's about transforming survival into a thriving, vibrant life as you build healthier relationships. This book is your tool, your guide, and your inspiration to rewrite your story, moving from a past defined by others to a future crafted by your design. Let's begin this journey together.

1

Foundations of Toxic Relationships

Have you ever felt like you're constantly walking on eggshells, second-guessing every decision, or feeling like you're never good enough, no matter how hard you try? These feelings might not just be a passing phase but could be signs of being in a toxic relationship. This chapter peels back the layers of what makes a relationship toxic, helping you to understand and recognize the underlying dynamics that differentiate these damaging interactions from healthy relationships. You're not alone in this—many have navigated this tumultuous terrain, and understanding these foundations is your first step toward healing and empowerment.

Defining Toxicity

A relationship is toxic when behaviors are emotionally and, sometimes, physically harmful to one party. It's essential to distinguish these relationships from those with occasional healthy conflicts. In a healthy relationship, disagreements are resolved through communication and compromise, and both individuals' needs are considered and respected. Conversely, toxic relationships often involve patterns of behavior that undermine one's sense of self-worth and wellbeing. These patterns may include pervasive criticism, disrespect, jealousy, stonewalling, and manipulation. The key here is consistency and intensity—while all relationships have their ups and downs, we define toxic relationships by an ongoing, unbalanced dynamic that wears down one's mental and emotional health.

Power Imbalance

At the heart of most toxic relationships is a significant power imbalance, where one person holds more control or influence over the emotional, physical, or financial wellbeing of the other. This imbalance can manifest through controlling behaviors, such as dictating who the other person can see, where they can go, or even how they should think and feel. Dependence is often a tool used to maintain this imbalance—financial dependence, emotional dependence, or social dependence. In many cases, the dominant individual will use tactics like guilt or intimidation to keep the other person in subjugation and uncertainty.

Emotional Impact

The emotional toll of being in a toxic relationship cannot be overstated. Constant exposure to a harmful environment can lead to diminished self-worth, chronic stress, anxiety, and depression. You might find yourself constantly anxious about your partner's mood swings, which can leave you perpetually on edge, disrupting your ability to focus, work, or enjoy life. The fear of triggering an adverse reaction creates a cycle where you always try to appease or please the other person, often at the cost of your own needs and happiness.

Cycle of Abuse

Understanding the cycle of abuse is crucial in recognizing and addressing toxic patterns. This cycle typically starts with tension building, where communication breaks down, and the victim feels a growing sense of dread and discomfort. An incident of verbal, emotional, or physical abuse follows this phase. Afterward, the abusive partner may enter a honeymoon phase, characterized by apologies, blame-shifting, or even gifts and loving gestures, only for the cycle to start again. It's this inconsistency and unpredictability that can be psychologically debilitating, making it hard for the victim to leave due to confusion, love, hope, and fear of escalation.

Recognizing these aspects of toxic relationships is the first step toward untangling yourself from their grip. As you continue to read, remember that understanding these dynamics is about gaining the tools and insights to navigate your way to safety and emotional health. You're taking back the power, one page at a time.

Gaslighting Unveiled

Gaslighting is a term that often surfaces in discussions about emotional abuse. Yet, its subtleties can make it hard to grasp and even harder to identify when you're the one experiencing it. Originally derived from the 1938 play and later a film titled "Gaslight," where a husband manipulates his wife to the point where she doubts her sanity, the term has come to describe a form of psychological manipulation where one person sows seeds of doubt in another, making them question their reality, memory, or perceptions. This tactic is profoundly damaging because it can erode trust and confidence, leaving individuals unsure of what they know and feel, questioning their judgment and reality.

Common tactics of gaslighting include outright denial by the abuser that certain events ever happened, contradicting your memories of events, and scoffing at your perceptions as overreactions or misinterpretations. They might also shift the blame to you, suggesting that you're making things up or are mistaken. This behavior can manifest in seemingly benign comments like, "You're too sensitive," or "You're imagining things." Still, over time, these micro-aggressions accumulate into a thick fog of confusion. Imagine consistently being told that your concerns are invalid or that the issues you raise are figments of your imagination. The impact is not just immediate confusion but a long-term erosion of self-trust.

The psychological effects of gaslighting are impactful. Victims may experience severe anxiety, becoming excessively worried about making mistakes or misremembering events, which can lead to paralysis in decision-making or extreme self-doubt. The constant second-guessing can lead to a mental state that borders on feeling insane because what you perceive doesn't align with what you are hearing. Over time, this persistent doubt can escalate to depression as you feel increasingly isolated in your unvalidated experiences, making the world seem inherently unstable and untrustworthy.

To counter act gaslighting, you have to start by recognizing the signs. Awareness is your shield; it helps you understand when someone questions your reality or dismiss your perceptions without a valid reason. Keep a journal of events and conversations —not just what was said, but also how it made you feel. This record can be a grounding tool to confirm your experiences and feelings when someone tries to distort them. Having trusted confidantes who can offer perspectives outside the gaslit relationship is also helpful. These allies can help affirm your reality and rebuild trust in your perceptions. Remember, reconnecting with your intuition is reclaiming your power from the gaslighter. This empowerment is about tuning back into your inner voice, often drowned out by the insidiousness of gaslighting.

Narcissism Explained: More Than Just Vanity

The term 'narcissism' often conjures images of self-absorption to the point of vanity. Still, the reality of encountering narcissism, especially in a relationship, extends far beyond someone merely obsessed with their reflection or social media presence. Narcissism, particularly when it edges into the territory of Narcissistic Personality Disorder (NPD), involves a complex array of behaviors that can deeply affect interpersonal relationships. It's crucial to distinguish between narcissistic traits—which many people may exhibit to some degree—and NPD, which is a diagnosable mental health condition characterized by persistent patterns of grandiosity, a constant need for admiration, and a lack of empathy.

Individuals with NPD often display behaviors that can be harmful to those around them. A lack of empathy, one of the hallmark signs of narcissism, means that they struggle to recognize or validate others' feelings and needs. This trait alone can lead to significant emotional distress for their partners or family members, who may feel perpetually sidelined, misunderstood, or unappreciated. Grandiosity manifests as an exaggerated sense of one's importance, which might lead a narcissist to believe they are superior and entitled to special treatment. This belief can result in unreasonable expectations and demands placed on those around them, setting the stage for conflict when these demands are not met or questioned.

Manipulation is another common tactic employed by those with narcissistic tendencies. These behaviors can include gaslighting, exploiting others to achieve personal gains, or using emotional withdrawal as a form of punishment or control. The person on the receiving end of such behaviors might find themselves constantly trying to appease the narcissist, often at the cost of their wellbeing and happiness. The impact of these behaviors on relationships can be devastating. Partners of narcissists often report feeling like they are living in a one-sided relationship where their needs are consistently made subordinate to the whims and fancies of their partner.

Protecting oneself from the negative effects of a narcissist's behavior starts with recognition and acknowledgment of the reality of the situation. It's common for those involved with narcissists to live in denial about the nature of their relationship. Admitting that a problem exists is a significant and often painful first step. Once you take this step, setting boundaries becomes crucial. Boundaries can be emotional, such as deciding what behavior you will not tolerate and sticking to it, or physical, such as limiting the time spent together or in certain situations.

Communication is key in enforcing these boundaries. Clear, assertive communication about your needs and expectations can help prevent misunderstandings and manipulative reinterpretations. Remember, when dealing with a narcissist, less is often more. Offering too much detail can give them ammunition to use against you later. Instead, keep your statements clear and concise. It's also beneficial to cultivate a support network of friends or professionals who understand narcissism and can offer both emotional support and reality checks against the narcissist's distortions.

Finally, prioritize self-care. Relationships with narcissists can be incredibly draining, leaving you feeling emotionally depleted. Be available for activities that replenish your energy and give you peace and fulfillment outside your challenging relationship dynamics. Whether it's pursuing a hobby, spending time in nature, or practicing meditation, taking care of your emotional and physical wellbeing gives you the strength to deal with the challenges of a relationship marked by narcissism. Remember, you cannot pour from an empty cup, and maintaining your health is essential for any confrontation with the demanding situations that arise when interacting with a narcissist.

Manipulation Tactics and How They Work

Manipulation in relationships can often be subtle and insidious, leaving you feeling confused, drained, and lacking control. It's not just about the occasional misleading comment or selfish behavior; it's a systematic approach one person uses to gain power, control, or compliance from another. Understanding these tactics can illuminate patterns you might have overlooked, allowing you to reclaim control of your interactions and emotional wellbeing.

One common manipulation tactic is **guilt-tripping**, where one person uses emotional responses to compel you to do something against your will. Imagine a scenario where you plan a quiet evening alone after a long week of work. However, your partner might express disappointment or sadness over your choice, suggesting that you do not care about spending time with them, thus leveraging your empathy and love to make you forgo your plans. This tactic plays on your emotions, turning them into tools of compliance. Another prevalent method is **isolation**, where the manipulator tries to cut you off from your support network. They might criticize your friends and family, subtly or overtly, or create scenarios that make social interactions unpleasant for you.

Breadcrumbing is yet another manipulative move in a toxic relationship. Consider this example.

Alex and Taylor have been casually dating for a few months. Alex constantly sends Taylor occasional text messages, flirty compliments, and emojis, giving the impression that they are interested and invested in the relationship. However, whenever

Taylor tries to take the relationship to a more serious level or seeks clarity about their future, Alex becomes evasive and avoids the conversation. This pattern continues with Alex giving Taylor just enough attention to keep him interested, but never fully committing or taking the relationship to the next level. This behavior leaves Taylor feeling confused, insecure, and hoping for more, while Alex maintains control and avoids any real emotional involvement. This is a classic example of breadcrumbing in a toxic relationship.

Over time, this can lead you to become more dependent on the person, increasing their influence and control over you.

The psychological principles behind these manipulation tactics are deeply rooted in exploiting emotional vulnerabilities. Cognitive dissonance, a state where your beliefs do not match your actions, is a common target. Manipulators often put you in situations where you must choose between your values and desires, creating psychological discomfort and confusion they can exploit by offering 'solutions' that serve their ends. Emotional dependency is another principle often exploited. By becoming the primary source of your emotional satisfaction, manipulators ensure that you continue to depend on them for your emotional needs, making it difficult to break away or challenge their authority.

Identifying your vulnerabilities to manipulation is vital. It requires honest self-reflection to understand why and how someone can manipulate you. Are you someone who struggles to say no because you fear conflict? Do you find yourself going to great lengths to avoid disappointing others? These traits are not flaws but aspects of your personality that someone may try to exploit in a toxic relationship. Recognizing these can help you understand situations where you might be more susceptible to manipulation.

Building resistance to manipulation involves several strategies, starting with setting firm boundaries. Boundaries are your rules and limits that define how you expect to be treated by others. Communicating these boundaries to your partner or anyone else is crucial, as is the consistency in enforcing them. It might feel uncomfortable initially, especially if confrontation has been something you've avoided, but maintaining these boundaries is essential for your mental health and self-respect.

Seeking external support plays a vital role in building resistance against manipulation. Turning to trusted friends, family members, or a professional can give you perspectives outside the manipulative relationship. These perspectives can affirm your feelings and thoughts when your partner is invalidating them within the relationship. Support groups or counseling can offer guidance and strategies to manage manipulation more effectively, helping you regain confidence in your judgments and decisions.

Understanding and resisting manipulation involve confronting the manipulator and rebuilding and fortifying one's sense of self. They involve recognizing the signs, understanding the psychological games, and actively protecting one's emotional and mental well-being. Remember, the goal is not just to counteract manipulation but to create a space where one's emotions and needs are respected and valued.

Psychological Effects of Long-Term Exposure to Toxicity

Living through a prolonged toxic relationship can deeply scar the psyche, often in ways that might not be immediately visible. The relentless stress and emotional turmoil can seep into your everyday experiences, altering how you perceive yourself and the world around you. The emotional and psychological wounds inflicted by sustained exposure to toxic environments are profound. They can persist long after the relationship has ended. These scars can manifest as persistent feelings of sadness, anxiety, or a pervasive sense of worthlessness, which can disrupt your ability to function and enjoy life. It's like carrying a backpack filled with stones — each day, the load does not lighten, affecting every step you take, every move you make.

The impact of these experiences can be so severe that they lead to conditions such as Post-Traumatic Stress Disorder (PTSD) or other stress-related disorders. Typically associated with survivors of intense physical or emotional trauma, PTSD can also occur in individuals who have endured long-term emotional abuse. Symptoms might include flashbacks of distressing incidents, nightmares, severe anxiety, and uncontrollable thoughts about the relationship. This condition can make you feel perpetually trapped in your past toxic experiences, unable to move forward, as if every day involves walking through a minefield of old fears and anxieties that might explode at the slightest touch.

Compounding the situation, those enduring these conditions might develop unhealthy coping mechanisms. These are often subconscious attempts to manage the overwhelming feelings of distress associated with their experiences. Some might turn to substance abuse — alcohol, prescription drugs, or other narcotics — as a temporary escape from pain. Others might withdraw from social interactions, driven by a fear of encountering situations that could trigger painful memories or emotions. This withdrawal can lead to isolation, which, while offering a haven from potential emotional triggers, also cuts off access to supportive relationships and experiences that could aid in recovery. It's as if you're building a wall to protect yourself, but the same wall also keeps out much of the sunlight.

As we move forward, it's crucial to understand that healing from these psychological effects is not only possible but also a pivotal part of reclaiming your life. The path to healing is multifaceted, involving self-reflection, professional therapy, and possibly medication to manage symptoms. It's about slowly dismantling the wall you've built — not by tearing it down all at once, but by removing one stone at a time, allowing more light to enter with each step. This process is gradual and often challenging, as it involves confronting painful memories and emotions. However, it is also a path filled with hope — a promise that the weights you carry you can lift, allowing you to move more freely and experience life more fully.

As you continue on this path, remember that healing is not linear. There might be days when the stones in your backpack feel heavier than usual, or when the walls you're dismantling seem to rebuild themselves overnight. These days, it's essential to show compassion and remind yourself that healing takes time. Each step forward, no matter how small, is a step towards a lighter backpack and a life where the past no longer holds you captive.

The Role of Self-Esteem in Attracting Toxic Partners

Self-esteem acts as the foundation upon which we build our relationships. It influences how we see ourselves and, crucially, how we believe we deserve to be treated by others. When self-esteem is low, it can create a vulnerability that may make one more susceptible to toxic relationships. Often, without realizing it, individuals with diminished self-esteem might find themselves drawn to partners who reinforce their negative self-perceptions. It's a painful irony that those who most need validation and respect are sometimes least likely to seek it in healthy ways. Instead, the familiarity of criticism or neglect resonates with their internal dialogue. This dialogue erroneously confirms they are unworthy of better treatment.

This susceptibility stems from a few core beliefs rooted in low self-esteem. If you believe you are unlovable, you might tolerate neglect or emotional abuse, thinking it's the best you can receive. If you see yourself as powerless, you might not resist controlling behavior, assuming it's normal for others to call the shots in your life. These patterns are not about a lack of intelligence or awareness, but deep-seated beliefs developed over time, often from childhood. Recognizing this is painful but essential in understanding how toxic relationships can perpetuate a cycle of diminished self-worth.

As these relationships progress, they often further erode self-esteem, creating a vicious cycle. Each episode of emotional abuse, each dismissive comment, chips away at self-worth even more, reinforcing the belief that you deserve no better. It's like being caught in a storm where every burst of wind and rain convinces you that you cannot hope for sunshine. Breaking free from this cycle is not just about leaving the toxic relationship but about fundamentally changing how you view yourself.

Rebuilding self-esteem starts with recognizing your inherent worth, independent of anyone else's opinion. This process can be challenging, especially if your self-view was shaped by years of belittlement or criticism. Begin by setting small, manageable goals that allow you to experience success and reaffirm your capabilities. Engage in activities that nurture your spirit and bring you joy, whether art, music, nature, or sports. These activities aren't just hobbies—they affirm your right to happiness and expressions of your unique self.

It's also important to surround yourself with positive influences. Seek out friends, family members, or groups that uplift you. In these environments, you can start seeing reflections of yourself full of potential and worth. Therapy can play a crucial role in this process, providing a safe space to explore and understand the roots of your self-esteem issues. A therapist can help you unpack the baggage of the past and give you tools to construct a more positive self-image.

As your self-esteem strengthens, you will likely find that your relationships naturally begin to change. You'll become better at setting boundaries and recognizing red flags. You'll start attracting and choosing partners who respect and enhance your self-worth. You aren't just about being selective; it's about being attracted to a different kind of energy. You'll find yourself gravitating towards supportive and kind people because you recognize that's what you deserve.

You can build healthy relationships on mutual respect, trust, and support. In such relationships, power is balanced, and communication is open. Partners encourage each other's growth rather than stifle it. When you know your value, you expect and demand these qualities in your relationships. You also contribute to a healthy relationship dynamic by approaching it from a place of strength and self-respect, not insecurity and neediness.

2

Identifying Toxicity in Various Relationships

A s we continue exploring the multifaceted world of toxic relationships, we focus on the romantic connections that often hold the deepest sway over our hearts and minds. With their intense bonds and emotional investments, romantic relationships can significantly impact our well-being. Recognizing the signs of toxicity within these relationships is not just about safeguarding our emotional health; it's about nurturing our capacity to love and be loved in the healthiest ways possible. You deserve a relationship that uplifts and supports you, and identifying toxic patterns is the first step in cultivating such connections.

Romantic Relationships Under the Microscope

Romantic Red Flags

In the landscape of love, certain red flags indicate the presence of toxicity. These signs can initially be subtle but become more apparent as the relationship progresses. One major red flag is constant criticism. Suppose your partner frequently criticizes your actions, appearance, or decisions, diminishing your self-esteem. In that case, it's a sign that the relationship is veering into toxic territory. Another significant indicator is control. Control can manifest as controlling your finances, dictating your social interactions, making decisions about your life without your input, or stonewalling. Stonewalling is when your partner withdraws from a conversation and refuses to respond as a means of control. Beyond occasional insecurities, jealousy can also be a red flag when it leads to possessive behaviors or unfounded accusations about your fidelity. These behaviors are not signs of love; they are markers of a relationship based on control and insecurity.

Intensity vs. Intimacy

It's crucial to differentiate between intensity and genuine intimacy in relationships. You can mistake intensity in a relationship for passion, but it often masks a lack of authentic connection. It's characterized by extreme highs and lows, with emotions swinging wildly from passionate love to intense arguments. Genuine intimacy, on the other hand, is built on a foundation of mutual respect, understanding, and consistent, supportive interaction. It involves a deep emotional connection that fosters a sense of security and trust, where both partners feel valued and heard. Intimacy grows over time and is characterized by stability and a deepening of emotional bonds rather than dramatic fluctuations in affection and attention.

Breaking the Cycle

Breaking the cycle of toxic romantic relationships begins with self-awareness and a commitment to your well-being. It involves recognizing the patterns that have led you into poisonous relationships and consciously choosing a different path. You may have to set stricter boundaries about acceptable behavior or seek professional help to understand your relationship dynamics better. It also involves cultivating self-worth outside of any romantic relationship. Engage in activities reinforcing your value and independence, such as pursuing personal interests or strengthening friendships and family ties. Remember, you can refuse to repeat cycles that no longer serve you.

Self-Worth in Romance

Your self-worth is critical in determining the kind of romantic relationships you engage in. When you value yourself, you set higher standards for how someone should treat you. You are more likely to leave relationships that don't meet these standards. Cultivating self-worth can involve affirmations, therapy, and practices like mindfulness that help you connect deeply with your intrinsic value. It's about realizing that you deserve respect and love that uplifts and supports, not diminishes. This self-recognition guides you in selecting healthier relationships and enriches your contributions to a relationship, making it more fulfilling and balanced.

Recognizing toxic patterns in romantic relationships is pivotal to emotional health and overall life satisfaction. As we delve deeper into these dynamics, remember that every step you take towards understanding and addressing these patterns is a step towards a healthier, happier you. You are learning to recognize harmful behaviors and setting the stage for more prosperous, rewarding relationships that honor your worth and nurture your growth.

When Family Ties Strangle: Navigating Toxic Relatives

Family dynamics are often complex, shaped by long histories and deep emotional ties. When these relationships become toxic, they can significantly impact your well-being due to the inherent expectations and the strong bonds that family members share. Toxic behaviors within families can vary widely but often include manipulation, constant criticism, or emotional neglect. These behaviors may stem from long-standing patterns or roles assigned within the family that no longer serve the individuals involved but persist out of tradition or habit. For example, a parent might have unrealistic expectations of success for their children, leading to constant pressure and criticism that undermines the child's confidence and self-perception. Alternatively, one sibling might always be labeled as the 'responsible one,' placing an unfair share of family responsibilities on their shoulders.

Setting boundaries within such deeply intertwined relationships requires both clarity and courage. Start by identifying specific behaviors that you find harmful. Articulating these can help you understand and communicate your needs more effectively. For instance, if a family member frequently calls you to unload their emotional distress without reciprocation or respect for your time, you might set a boundary by specifying times you are available to talk or suggesting they seek support from a professional therapist. Communicating these boundaries directly and calmly is critical and using "I" statements that focus on your feelings and needs for example, "I am feeling cornered. I need you to back up a bit." rather than accusatory "you" statements such as, "You look like you want to trap me in this corner." might lead to defensiveness or conflict.

Dealing with the guilt often accompanying setting boundaries with family can be particularly challenging. This guilt usually stems from deeply ingrained beliefs about family obligations or fear of being seen as selfish or uncaring. Recognizing that setting boundaries is necessary for healthy relationships and self-care is essential. Reminding yourself that you are not responsible for another adult's emotional well-being and that everyone has the right to protect their mental health can help alleviate some of this guilt. Additionally, consider the long-term benefits of setting boundaries, not only for your well-being but also for the relationship's health. Boundaries often help prevent resentment and burnout, making interactions more genuine and less fraught with obligatory tension.

Seeking support outside the family structure can also be invaluable as you navigate these challenges. Support groups, friends, or a therapist can offer perspectives and validation not influenced by familial bias or history. These external inputs can be crucial in helping you see your situation more clearly and supporting you in maintaining your boundaries. They can provide a safe space to express feelings and frustrations you may feel uncomfortable sharing with family members. Moreover, external support can help bridge understanding in ways that internal family efforts cannot by providing neutral mediation or alternative coping strategies that family members might not have considered.

Navigating toxic relationships within a family requires a delicate balance of assertiveness and empathy, understanding and firmness. By setting clear boundaries, managing guilt, and seeking external support, you can protect your emotional health and potentially lead toward healthier family dynamics. Remember, changing deep-seated family patterns takes time, and setbacks are part of the process. Patience and self-compassion are your allies as you work through these familial challenges.

Toxic Friendships: Recognizing Frenemies

Friendships are meant to enrich our lives, offering companionship, support, and joy. However, not all friendships fulfill these positive roles. Some can evolve into or begin as toxic relationships that drain your emotional energy and undermine your self-esteem. Identifying these toxic friendships involves recognizing clear signs, such as persistent one-sidedness, where you always give time, energy, or emotional support without receiving much in return. Another sign can be jealousy, not the fleeting kind spurred by specific events, but a constant undercurrent that taints the joy in your achievements and milestones. Such jealousy might manifest in subtle put-downs or backhanded compliments that leave you questioning your friend's sincerity. Other indicators include:

- Consistent negativity.
- Lack of respect for your boundaries.
- Feelings of dread rather than excitement at spending time with them.

These signs point to an imbalance that can make the friendship feel more like a burden than a mutual exchange of affection and support.

Although necessary, letting go of toxic friends can be challenging. It often requires a firm resolve and a clear understanding of the reasons behind your decision. Begin by reducing the time and energy you invest in these relationships. You might decline invitations more often or opt for group settings when interaction is unavoidable, thus diluting the intensity of one-on-one time. Communication is also vital in this process. If comfortable and safe, express your feelings about the friendship dynamics to the other person, focusing on specific behaviors rather than general accusations. For instance, instead of saying, "You're always so negative," you might say, "I feel drained when our conversations focus heavily on negative topics," which clearly states your feelings without assigning blame. In cases where direct conversation might lead to confrontation or further toxicity, gradually distancing yourself may be the safest and most effective approach. Remember, it's essential to prioritize your mental health and well-being over maintaining a friendship that leaves you feeling undervalued and unhappy.

In contrast, supportive friendships form the foundation of mutual respect, trust, and positive regard. Supportive relationships are characterized by a healthy give and take, where both parties feel valued and supported. Cultivating such friendships involves actively seeking out individuals who share similar values and interests and demonstrate emotional maturity and respect for others. It's also crucial to be the kind of friend you seek. Be attentive, respectful, and supportive; listen without always offering advice and celebrate others' successes without envy. Engaging in activities and groups that align with your interests can increase your chances of meeting potential friends who will add positive value to your life. Remember, quality always trumps quantity when it comes to friendships. A few solid and supportive relationships are far more enriching than numerous superficial ones.

Leaving toxic friendships behind often opens new avenues for personal growth. Freed from unhealthy relationships' negativity and emotional drain, you might have more energy and enthusiasm to invest in previously neglected pursuits. Now can be an ideal time to explore new interests or revisit old hobbies that you had set aside. Distancing yourself from toxic friendships can also lead to greater self-awareness and an improved ability to set and maintain boundaries. These are invaluable skills that will serve you well in all areas of life, enhancing your interactions not just in personal relationships but also in professional settings.

Most importantly, overcoming the challenges of toxic friendships can bolster your confidence in your ability to manage difficult situations, affirming your strength and resilience. As you navigate this transition, allow yourself to embrace the freedom and opportunities of letting go of relationships that do not serve your best interests. Embracing this new space can significantly enhance your emotional and mental well-being, leading to a more fulfilled and balanced life.

Workplace Woes: Dealing with Toxicity in Professional Settings

Navigating the complexities of a work environment can be challenging, especially when toxicity permeates the air. A toxic work environment often manifests through consistent negative behaviors and practices that can significantly undermine employee morale and productivity. A lack of support and communication from management, pervasive negativity, unfair treatment, and a general atmosphere of disrespect typically mark these environments. Employees might experience regular undermining by superiors or colleagues, face discriminatory remarks, or be subjected to unrealistic pressures without adequate resources or recognition. The cumulative effect of these factors can lead to increased stress, decreased job satisfaction, and, in severe cases, burnout or mental health declines. Just as a plant struggles to thrive in poor soil, even the most dedicated employees can find it difficult to maintain productivity and commitment in such draining circumstances.

Managing toxic coworkers and bosses requires tact and strategic planning. The first step is often to establish clear personal boundaries. Decide what behaviors you will not tolerate and communicate these limits calmly and professionally. For instance, if a coworker consistently interrupts you in meetings, you might say, "I value your enthusiasm, but I would appreciate it if you could let me finish my points before responding." Documentation can become your ally when dealing with a toxic boss. Keep records of interactions you believe cross the line, noting the conversations' dates, times, and details. This record can be invaluable if you must escalate the issue to human resources or seek external advice. It's also beneficial to seek allies within the workplace—colleagues who share your experiences or perspectives can offer support and may join you in addressing the issues if they are also affected.

Maintaining professionalism in such settings is a must, not just for your career prospects but for your mental well-being. It would help if you concentrated on managing your reactions to toxic behaviors. While feeling upset or defensive is natural, responding in kind can exacerbate the situation and potentially harm your professional reputation. Instead, focus on answering in ways that uphold your integrity and professionalism. You may need to compose yourself before responding to a provocative comment or addressing issues through formal channels rather than in the heat of the moment. Maintaining professionalism also means knowing when to seek support from human resources or trusted mentors within your organization who can provide guidance and support.

Recognizing when to move on from a toxic work environment is a crucial skill. It often comes down to assessing the impact of the environment on your health and professional growth. If you dread working each day, experience significant stress or health issues, or notice a stall in your professional development, these might be signs that the environment is no longer conducive to your growth. Before deciding to leave, consider whether there are avenues for change within the organization, such as transferring to a different department or speaking to higher-ups about the issues. If these routes are exhausted or unavailable, consider seeking new opportunities where your skills and contributions can be appreciated, and your professional growth can continue unimpeded.

In the professional realm, understanding and addressing toxicity can profoundly affect your career trajectory and personal well-being. As you move forward, remember that while you may not always control the environment, you do control your responses and decisions. Each choice to address, adapt to, or move away from toxicity is a step toward cultivating a healthier professional path that aligns with your values and career aspirations.

The Subtleties of Toxicity in LGBTQIA+ Relationships

Navigating relationships can be inherently complex, and for those in the LGBTQIA+ community, these complexities often multiply due to unique societal and personal challenges. Broader issues of discrimination and acceptance can sometimes overshadow the nuances of toxic relationships within the LGBTQIA+ spectrum. Yet, they require equal, if not greater, attention due to their profound impact on individuals' lives. Understanding these peculiarities helps not only in recognizing toxic patterns but also in fostering supportive environments where individuals feel valued and understood.

The unique challenges faced by LGBTQIA+ individuals in toxic relationships often stem from a layered intersection of societal pressure, internalized homophobia, and the stigmatization of their identities. These factors can create a fertile ground for toxicity to thrive. For instance, the fear of losing social acceptance might lead someone to tolerate unhealthy behaviors from a partner who accepts their sexual or gender identity. Similarly, internalized negative beliefs about one's identity can make individuals undeserving of healthy, loving relationships, which may lead them to seek or stay in harmful situations. Moreover, the smaller size of potential dating pools in some areas can make LGBTQIA+ individuals feel pressured to remain in unhealthy relationships due to a fear of loneliness or lack of alternatives.

In such contexts, the importance of supportive communities becomes unmistakable. These communities offer a backdrop against which individuals can see reflections of their worth and potential for happiness. They provide camaraderie and understanding, practical advice, and examples of healthy

LGBTQIA+ relationships that might not be visible in mainstream culture. Finding and engaging with community groups, whether online or in person, can be incredibly empowering. These groups often organize events, provide resources, and foster safe spaces where individuals can share their experiences and learn from others without fear of judgment or misunderstanding. They also serve as crucial support networks when navigating the process of leaving or recovering from toxic relationships, offering both emotional support and practical assistance.

The stigma associated with seeking help for relationship problems can be particularly pronounced for LGBTQIA+ individuals, who may already feel marginalized or misunderstood by mainstream support systems. Overcoming this stigma is crucial, as it can prevent many from accessing the help they need to escape toxic dynamics. It's important to advocate for and utilize LGBTQIA+-affirming therapy and counseling services that offer specialized understanding and support. These services are not only more likely to provide relevant and empathetic assistance. Still, they can also help individuals address and dismantle the layers of internalized stigma that might have made them vulnerable to toxicity in their relationships.

Affirming one's self-identity is a powerful counteraction to the dynamics of a toxic relationship. It involves embracing and celebrating your identity despite external opinions or pressures. This self-affirmation is a radical act of self-love that strengthens personal boundaries and clarifies unacceptable behaviors or attitudes. It can also inspire confidence to make necessary changes in one's life, including ending toxic relationships. Engaging in activities that reinforce your identity, such as participating in LGBTQIA+ events, consuming media that reflects your experiences, or simply expressing yourself in ways that feel true to your identity, can bolster your self-esteem, and reduce the influence of toxic partners.

Nurturing a strong sense of self within a supportive community environment provides a robust foundation from which individuals can confront and overcome the challenges posed by toxic relationships. By focusing on these areas, LGBTQIA+ individuals can not only navigate the complexities of their relationships with more clarity and confidence but also contribute to a broader culture of respect and dignity within their communities, paving the way for healthier and more fulfilling connections.

Digital Dangers: Identifying Toxicity in Online Interactions

In today's interconnected world, our digital interactions can be just as impactful as our face-to-face ones, sometimes even blurring the lines between the two. Understanding how toxicity manifests online is crucial as it can subtly infiltrate our daily lives, often without the precise boundaries and physical cues guiding real-world interactions. Online toxicity can take many forms, from cyberbullying and harassment to subtler forms of negative interactions like trolling or passive-aggressive comments on social media. These behaviors can create a hostile, intimidating, or just plain uncomfortable environment. The anonymity and distance of digital platforms can encourage individuals to say things they might not in person, amplifying their words' intensity and impact. Recognizing these signs is the first step in protecting oneself from the pervasive spread of online negativity.

Developing a proactive digital wellness strategy is essential to safeguard oneself from online toxicity. The strategies should include:

- Being selective about who you connect with or follow online.
- Curating your social media feeds to minimize exposure to harmful content.

- Utilizing privacy settings to control who can see and interact with your posts.

Engaging in online environments that foster positivity and support rather than negativity and criticism can also significantly enhance your online experience. When harassment occurs, most platforms have mechanisms for reporting abusive content or blocking users. Using these tools can help create a safer online space. Additionally, being mindful of how much personal information you share online can prevent manipulative or harmful uses of your data. Remember, every layer of defense you add can function as a buffer, preserving your peace of mind and emotional well-being.

The impact of social media on our mental health and relationships is profound and multifaceted. While these platforms can offer incredible ways to connect, share, and learn, they can also lead to feelings of inadequacy, anxiety, and depression if not managed carefully. The curated portrayals of success and happiness often seen on social media can distort our perceptions of our lives, leading to dissatisfaction and a constant feeling of lacking. Furthermore, the immediacy and permanency of online interactions can lead to impulsive behaviors that may damage real-life relationships. For instance, venting about a partner or friend online can hurt the individual's feelings and escalate personal conflicts into public spectacles. Balancing the way we interact online and understanding its impact on our mental health is crucial. It involves recognizing when social media use contributes to stress or unhappiness and mitigating this, such as setting time limits for daily use or taking regular digital detoxes.

Creating healthy digital boundaries is one of the most effective ways to protect your mental health in the digital age. This involves setting limits on how and when you use digital devices and defining clear guidelines for the interactions you are willing to engage in online. For example, you might decide not to respond to communications during certain hours to ensure you have time to unwind and disconnect from the digital world, or you might choose not to engage with anonymous accounts that display a pattern of negative interactions. Educating yourself and others about the importance of respectful and constructive communication online can also contribute to a more positive digital environment. Encourage discussions about digital etiquette and the real-world impact of online interactions within your community or circle. By fostering respect and thoughtfulness, we can collectively enhance our digital spaces, making them more prosperous and more supportive extensions of our real-world interactions.

As we navigate the complexities of our digital lives, we must remember that our online interactions can significantly affect our real-world experiences. By recognizing the signs of toxicity online, protecting ourselves with proactive strategies, understanding the psychological impacts, and establishing robust digital boundaries, we can take control of our digital interactions. This empowerment enhances our online experiences and enriches our overall quality of life, ensuring that our digital engagements are sources of joy, growth, and connection rather than stress and conflict. As we move forward, let's carry the lessons learned from navigating these digital landscapes and apply them to broader aspects of our online and offline relationships and interactions.

3

The Cycle of Toxicity

Y ou may wonder why specific relationship patterns repeat despite your best intentions in the quiet moments between the chaos of our daily lives. It's as if you're on a carousel that stops only to let you off at the same point where you began. This chapter is dedicated to understanding this cycle of toxicity that traps so many, delving into the roots that tether you to repetitive harmful interactions, and offering strategies to break free and forge a path to healthier relational landscapes.

Understanding Why We Repeat Toxic Patterns

Root Causes

At the core of recurring toxic relationship patterns are often unexamined root causes that drive our decisions, sometimes subconsciously. These roots can be multifaceted, intertwining past emotional injuries, learned behaviors from childhood, societal influences, or even past relationship traumas. For instance, if you grew up in a home where love was conditional—only shown in return for achievement or compliance—you might unwittingly seek similar dynamics in adulthood, equating love with needing approval or acceptance.

Another profound influence is the model of relationships witnessed during early development. If you saw one parent consistently dominating another, this dynamic may become your blueprint for relationships. It's not the love you're replicating; it's the familiarity of the pattern, mistaken for a known, albeit uncomfortable, comfort. These deep-seated beliefs and the behaviors they spawn are often veiled, making them easier to identify and address with introspective work.

Awareness as the First Step

Illuminating these patterns is akin to turning on a light in a long-darkened room. The shadows of past hurts and learned behaviors become visible, and only then can they be confronted. Awareness is your first tool in breaking the cycle of toxicity. It involves stepping back from your current experiences and examining them critically yet compassionately. Ask yourself: What makes you feel familiar with this situation? Have I felt like this before in other relationships? What role am I playing, and why does it feel scripted?

This self-reflection can be challenging; it often requires revisiting painful memories or acknowledging uncomfortable truths about your behavior. However, this process is crucial for change. It allows you to begin dismantling the harmful patterns you've been replicating, providing a clearer vision of the relationship dynamics you truly desire and deserve.

Breaking the Cycle

Once you know the toxic patterns you're repeating, the next step is active intervention. Breaking the cycle requires both courage and action. Start by setting new standards for your relationships. Communicate your needs clearly and assertively, not as demands but as necessary boundaries for your well-being. For example, if you always appease others at the expense of your happiness, practice saying no to small things first. Build up your confidence in asserting your needs before tackling more significant issues.

Creating an environment conducive to healthier relationships is also essential. Surround yourself with supportive friends who model the type of interactions you aspire to have. Their healthy behaviors can serve as a guide for your own. Additionally, diversify your sources of emotional fulfillment. Engage in activities that boost your self-esteem and independence, so your well-being doesn't hinge solely on your relationships.

Seeking Professional Help

Sometimes, the roots of toxic patterns are deep and tangled, making them challenging to untangle alone. In such cases, professional help from a counselor or therapist can be invaluable. These experts can help you identify the nuances of your behaviors and the underlying causes in a structured, supportive setting. Therapy can provide tailored strategies to alter these patterns, supplemented by professional insights and objective feedback. For many, therapy is a cornerstone of change, offering a safe space to heal and grow beyond the confines of past relationship dynamics.

Incorporating these strategies into your life doesn't just alter your relational orbits; it transforms them. By understanding the root causes, raising your awareness, actively breaking the cycle, and possibly seeking professional guidance, you equip yourself with the tools to stop the carousel of toxicity and step off into healthier, more fulfilling relationships. This transformative process isn't just about avoiding toxic relationships; it's about creating a life that celebrates and nurtures your worth, one step at a time.

The Role of Childhood Trauma in Adult Toxic Relationships

The shadows that follow us from childhood into adulthood are often subtle and deeply ingrained within our psyche, influencing our behaviors and choices without conscious awareness. A significant aspect of these shadows is childhood trauma, which can profoundly predispose individuals to toxic relationships later in life. Understanding this link is crucial for anyone looking to break free from such patterns and foster healthier, more fulfilling relationships.

Childhood trauma, in its many forms—whether emotional, physical, or psychological—creates a blueprint for how we view relationships and what we consider to be 'normal' or acceptable behavior from others. If children experience neglect, they might grow up feeling that they need to earn affection and attention, making them vulnerable to partners who withhold affection conditionally. Similarly, suppose a child is exposed to abuse. In that case, they might learn to associate love with pain, believing that volatile relationships filled with highs and lows are standard. These early experiences shape our attachment styles and influence how we relate to others, often pushing us towards partners who, unfortunately, mirror the toxic dynamics we are familiar with from our youth.

Healing these childhood wounds is a process that requires patience, persistence, and, often, professional guidance. The first step is recognizing these early experiences' impact on your current relationship patterns. This realization can be painful, as it involves revisiting some of the darkest chapters of your life and acknowledging their effects on your present. However, this recognition is also empowering—it marks the beginning of choosing something different for yourself.

The healing process often involves revisiting these childhood experiences and reprocessing them to reduce their emotional hold over you. Therapy can be particularly beneficial in this regard. Techniques like Cognitive Behavioral Therapy (CBT) can help you reframe the negative beliefs about yourself that were formed during childhood, while therapies like Eye Movement Desensitization and Reprocessing (EMDR) can reduce the distress associated with traumatic memories. In some cases, participating in supportive group therapy can be advantageous, as it helps you realize that you are not alone in your experiences, providing a collective validation that is incredibly healing.

Professional Interventions

Professional interventions can vary widely, each suited to the specific needs and experiences of the individual. For someone grappling with the effects of childhood trauma, finding a therapist who specializes in trauma recovery can be transformative. These professionals are equipped with the tools to help you navigate your past experiences safely and effectively, ensuring you do not have to revisit these painful memories alone. Moreover, they can offer personalized strategies tailored to your specific circumstances, which is crucial because healing is not a one-size-fits-all process.

For many, therapy might also include family counseling, particularly if the relationships within the family unit continue to perpetuate toxic patterns. Family therapy can help to address and mend the family dynamics that may have contributed to your trauma, fostering a healthier environment that supports the healing of all members. Additionally, for those who might find traditional one-on-one therapy daunting or inaccessible, online therapy platforms have become a viable alternative, providing flexibility and access to a wide range of therapeutic services from the comfort of your home.

Self-Compassion and Healing

In the journey of healing childhood wounds, self-compassion is a critical companion. It involves treating yourself with the same kindness, concern, and support you would offer a good friend. Healing from trauma is not a linear process; there are often setbacks and days when old patterns resurface. During these times, self-compassion allows you to navigate these challenges without harsh self-judgment, recognizing that setbacks are part of the healing process, not failure indicators.

Practicing self-compassion can include:

- Simple actions like speaking to yourself kindly.
- Acknowledging your progress.
- Allowing yourself space to feel and express your emotions safely.

It also involves setting realistic expectations for your healing process and recognizing the courage it takes to face your past and seek a better future. Remember, each step taken toward healing, no matter how small, is a testament to your strength and resilience.

As you continue to navigate the complexities of healing from childhood trauma, remember that this process is not just about moving away from past pain but also moving toward a future filled with healthier relationships and a deeper understanding of yourself. Each day provides a new opportunity to heal, grow, and redefine what love, and relationships mean to you, free from the shadows of the past.

Breaking Free: Ending the Cycle of Abuse

When the decision crystallizes in your mind to break free from the cycle of abuse, it marks a pivotal moment in your life. It's not merely about leaving a situation that harms you but about reclaiming your sense of self and right to a life marked by respect and kindness. Empowerment and agency are your allies in this journey, serving as the foundation upon which you can begin to rebuild a life free from the constraints of toxicity. To feel empowered is to recognize that you possess the ability to influence your life's direction and that you are not doomed to remain in harmful cycles indefinitely. Reclaiming agency involves taking proactive steps to assert control over your life choices and actions, even when external circumstances seem overwhelmingly oppressive.

Creating a support network is an essential step in breaking free. This network can include friends, family members, colleagues, or professionals who understand your situation and offer emotional and practical support. Start by identifying individuals who have shown empathy and understanding in the past. Reach out to them, share your plans, and express what kind of support you need— someone to listen to you, help with planning or provide a temporary place to stay. In addition to personal connections, consider seeking support groups for individuals who have experienced similar situations. These groups offer the dual benefit of emotional support and practical advice, providing both a sounding board and a repository of collective wisdom on overcoming your challenges.

Having a practical exit plan is crucial when you are ready to leave a toxic relationship. This plan should address immediate safety, financial stability, and legal considerations. Begin by securing your documents and valuables, setting aside emergency funds, and finding a safe place to stay. Consult a lawyer to understand your rights and legal options, mainly if marital assets or custody issues are involved. Changing passwords and updating security settings on your digital devices is also wise to protect your privacy. On a more personal level, prepare yourself emotionally for the change. Remind yourself why you are taking these steps and visualize the life you are working towards—a life free from abuse and filled with potential.

As you are looking towards your future beyond the act of leaving, it's essential to cultivate a hopeful perspective on life after abuse. Breaking free reveals a landscape filled with possibilities previously overshadowed by toxicity. It's a chance to rediscover and redefine who you are outside of the constraints imposed by an abusive relationship. Engage with activities and communities that align with your interests and values. Consider pursuing new or neglected aspirations, whether they involve career goals, hobbies, or education. Each step you take in rebuilding your life reinforces your independence and strengthens your belief in your ability to thrive. Remember, while the scars of abuse may not disappear overnight, they do not define your future. With each day that passes, you are not just surviving; you are actively constructing a new reality grounded in self-respect and genuine freedom.

The Science of Attachment and Toxic Relationships

Understanding the intricacies of attachment theory is akin to decoding the language of human connections. This theory, first developed by psychologist John Bowlby, posits that the nature of the bonds we form early in life with our caregivers influences our interpersonal relationships into adulthood. These early interactions set the groundwork for our attachment styles, blueprints for how we relate to others. In the context of toxic relationships, attachment theory offers a lens through which we can view our vulnerabilities and strengths in relational dynamics.

Attachment styles are generally categorized into secure, anxious, avoidant, and disorganized, each presenting distinct traits that affect how individuals perceive and react in relationships. A secure attachment style, characterized by a healthy balance of intimacy and independence, fosters relationships built on trust and mutual respect. Conversely, those with anxious or avoidant attachment styles may find themselves repeatedly entangled in toxic dynamics. For instance, someone with an anxious attachment style might perpetually fear abandonment and thus tolerate excessive negativity or control in a relationship to avoid being alone. Meanwhile, those with an avoidant attachment might push away closeness and perpetuate a cycle of emotional distance and misunderstanding.

The influence of these attachment styles on relationship dynamics is profound. They dictate how we respond to intimacy and conflict and how we communicate our needs and expectations. An individual with an avoidant attachment style, for example, might struggle to articulate their need for space, leading their partner to feel rejected or unloved, which can escalate tensions and misunderstandings. Recognizing your attachment style can provide critical insights into your role in toxic relationships, offering clues on why specific patterns feel so inescapable.

Changing entrenched attachment patterns can be challenging but possible. It begins with awareness—identifying your attachment style and understanding how it interacts with others around you. This awareness is the first step toward fostering healthier ways of connecting with partners. Cognitive-behavioral therapy (CBT) and other therapeutic modalities can be particularly effective in this regard, as they provide strategies to alter thought patterns and behaviors that stem from problematic attachment styles. For example, therapy can help someone with an anxious attachment style develop better self-soothing techniques, reducing their dependency on the emotional availability of their partner for their sense of worth.

Seeking secure attachments involves both an internal and external journey. Internally, it requires building self-awareness and self-esteem to feel deserving of healthy relationships. Externally, it consists of choosing partners with qualities conducive to secure attachment, such as consistency, availability, and responsiveness. Relationships in which both partners strive for a secure attachment can promote mutual growth and emotional satisfaction. Such relationships are characterized by partners who support each other's individuality while providing a dependable and nurturing connection.

As you navigate toward securing healthier attachments, remember that this process is about avoiding toxic relationships and creating a foundation for positive, loving interactions that enrich your life. It's about rewriting your relational blueprint to align with your emotional health and relationship goals. This endeavor enhances your romantic relationships and improves your interactions with friends, family, and even colleagues, broadening your capacity for empathy and deepening your interpersonal connections. Embracing this understanding of attachment styles illuminates paths to nurturing the fulfilling relationships you deserve, guiding your steps with the wisdom of psychological science.

Rebuilding Trust in Yourself and Others

After enduring the hardships of toxic relationships, one of the most profound challenges you might face is restoring your trust in others and yourself. Trust is the cornerstone of all healthy relationships; it's the soil from which love and understanding grow. Yet, rebuilding trust can feel like an uphill battle against doubt and past hurts when trust has been compromised, as often happens in toxic dynamics. However, understanding that this process is not just possible but essential for your emotional health and relational well-being is the first step toward healing.

The importance of rebuilding trust in oneself cannot be overstated. In the aftermath of toxic relationships, you may no longer have confidence in your judgment. You might question your ability to make sound decisions or worry about repeating past mistakes. This self-doubt manifests as a hesitation in trusting your feelings and instincts, critical tools for navigating future relationships and making healthy choices. To begin restoring this self-trust, start by affirming your experiences. Acknowledge that the feelings and intuitions you had during those toxic times were valid and perhaps were signals that something was amiss. By validating your past feelings, you reinforce the trust in your emotional responses.

It's also essential to reflect on your decisions that had positive outcomes, even during those challenging times. Perhaps you set a boundary, left an unhealthy situation, or sought help. Celebrating these choices can bolster your confidence in your decision-making abilities. Engaging in self-care practices that foster mental clarity and emotional stability can also help. Activities like meditation, journaling, or therapy can provide you with tools to understand better and trust your emotional responses, reinforcing the belief that you can protect and nurture yourself.

Trusting others again is another critical aspect of your healing journey. The betrayal and manipulation inherent in toxic relationships can lead to a guarded heart, making it difficult to open up to new connections. The fear of being hurt again might seem impossible at times. However, embracing vulnerability with appropriate boundaries can be a powerful pathway to rebuilding trust. Start with small steps, allowing yourself to trust in low-risk situations and building up to more significant ones. For instance, share a personal opinion or preference with someone and observe their reaction. If they respect your viewpoint, it can gradually lay the groundwork for deeper trust.

As you navigate these interactions, it's crucial to identify signs that indicate a relationship is trustworthy. Consistency is one of the primary indicators. People who are consistent in their words and actions are more likely to be reliable. Transparency is another crucial sign; individuals who are open about their thoughts and feelings and communicate openly tend to be trustworthy. Also, look for respect for boundaries. A person who acknowledges and respects your limits values your needs and will likely be a dependable part of your life.

Building healthy, trusting relationships involves actively engaging with people who demonstrate these trustworthy behaviors. It requires clear communication from the start. When you clearly express your needs, expectations, and boundaries, you set the tone for a relationship grounded in mutual respect and trust. It's also essential to be the kind of partner you seek. As you look for honesty, consistency, and respect in others, strive to embody these qualities yourself. This mutual exchange fosters an environment where trust can thrive.

Watch for red flags or behaviors that echo past toxic patterns in your interactions. Addressing these concerns early on can prevent misunderstandings and ensure the relationship stays healthy. Building trust is not about guaranteeing that you will never be hurt again—no relationship can offer that certainty. Instead, it's about equipping yourself with the knowledge and skills to enter into relationships with openness and mindfulness, balanced with the wisdom gained from past experiences. This balanced approach enhances your current relationships and enriches your overall quality of life, allowing you to connect with others in meaningful and fulfilling ways.

The Power of Resilience: Stories of Breaking Free

Resilience is often the ability to bounce back from setbacks. Still, in the context of toxic relationships, it encompasses so much more. It involves enduring, learning, and ultimately thriving despite the emotional adversities. This strength doesn't just help you survive the ordeals; it transforms you, enabling you to emerge wiser, stronger, and more empowered. Resilience in this light is not about returning to your original form but growing into someone more formidable and enlightened than before the challenges.

The stories of individuals who have navigated their way out of toxic relationships are not just narratives of escape but are testaments to human resilience. Take the example of Maya, who, after years in a manipulative relationship, found herself doubting her worth and sanity. Her journey of resilience began with the smallest affirmation of her feelings and experiences, which she journaled every night. Simple yet powerful written words became the seeds from which her new self-perception as deserving and capable grew. Over time, Maya's resilience saw her leaving the relationship and becoming a counselor to help others recognize and escape similar situations. Then there's the story of James, who endured years of emotional abuse. His resilience involved rekindling his passion for painting, a hobby he had set aside to appease his controlling partner. James rediscovered his voice and identity through his art, each stroke on the canvas reinforcing his journey from victim to survivor to a thriving artist now celebrated in community galleries.

Building personal resilience is not an overnight achievement but a gradual process of accumulating strength and wisdom. It starts with acknowledging and embracing your vulnerabilities. Recognizing that vulnerability does not equate to being weak but human and natural can significantly shift your perspective. It's also about cultivating a mindset that views challenges as opportunities to learn and grow. Cultivating a positive mindset involves changing your internal dialogues from "Why is this happening to me?" to "What can I learn from this experience?" Another vital component is setting healthy boundaries that honor your needs and values. These boundaries act as safeguards against toxicity and as affirmations of your self-worth.

Moreover, you can reinforce resilience through connections with supportive individuals who validate your feelings and experiences. Whether it's trusted friends, family, or support groups, these relationships provide comfort and perspective, reminding you that you're not alone in your struggles. Engaging in activities that boost your physical and emotional well-being, such as exercise, meditation, or hobbies, also builds resilience by improving your mood and reducing stress. No matter how small, each positive action you take contributes to a stronger, more resilient self.

Resilience is indeed a powerful pathway to personal empowerment and thriving post-toxicity. It equips you with the emotional tools to navigate future relationships more wisely and assertively. By transforming your adversities into strength and wisdom, resilience paves the way to survive past ordeals and thrive in new beginnings. Embracing resilience means embracing a life where past pains are not roadblocks but steppingstones to a more empowered and fulfilling existence.

As we close this chapter, remember that resilience is not inherent but cultivated. It's a choice and commitment to rise above your circumstances and emerge unscathed and enhanced. The stories shared here, including Maya's and James's, are not anomalies but possibilities—real-life proof that with resilience, breaking free from toxicity is just the beginning of a larger, more vibrant journey. By nurturing resilience, you equip yourself to face future challenges with a fortified spirit and an open heart, ready to embrace not just the absence of toxicity but the presence of genuine fulfillment and joy. This foundation of resilience sets the stage for healthier personal relationships. It enriches your interactions across all aspects of life, making resilience a tool for recovery and a cornerstone of a thriving existence.

As we transition to the next chapter, let's carry forward the resilience cultivated here, applying it to our personal lives and all arenas where we seek growth, understanding, and fulfillment. In doing so, we continue to build upon our foundation, exploring further how to survive and flourish in every aspect of our lives.

4

Preparing to Leave

When the whispers of dawn herald a new day, many of us relish its promise. But for those entwined in toxic relationships, each sunrise might seem to mock with a light that appears just out of reach, obscured by the shadows of turmoil. If you find yourself in such a relationship, know that the light isn't a cruel illusion—it's a beacon of hope, guiding you towards a horizon of safety and new beginnings. Preparing to leave a toxic relationship is an act of profound bravery and self-respect. You declare that you deserve better, and it's the crucial first step towards reclaiming your life.

Safety First: Creating a Plan to Leave

Assessing Risk

Before entering the sunlight, you must navigate the darkest part of the night. Assessing the risk involved in leaving a toxic relationship is this dark part—it's daunting but essential. Ask yourself how your partner typically reacts to boundaries or signs of independence. Their past responses can offer critical insights into potential risks. Consider the severity and frequency of emotional, verbal, or physical abuse you face. High-risk situations require meticulous planning, possibly involving authorities or professional help. Remember, acknowledging the gravity of your situation is not an act of fear but a strategic first step in safeguarding your journey.

Safety Plan Basics

A safety plan is your roadmap out of the shadows, tailored to guide you through the escape with meticulous care. This plan includes identifying safe places to stay, such as a friend's home, a family member's house, or a shelter. Have a list of emergency contacts—people who understand your situation and are ready to help immediately. Include local authorities, domestic abuse helplines, and trusted friends or relatives in this list. Pack an emergency bag with documents, clothing, medications, and necessary personal items. Keep this bag in a secure, quickly accessible place. Planning your exit route and transportation is also crucial; determine the safest time to leave and the safest mode of transport available.

Confidentiality is Key

The success of your plan often hinges on its confidentiality. The less the abuser knows about your intentions and details, the safer your exit will be. Avoid written notes or digital traces that could reveal your plans. Use secure, private methods to research or communicate with others about your departure. Consider using a computer at a local library or a friend's phone to look up information or communicate. The element of surprise can significantly enhance your safety during departure.

Utilizing Resources

You don't have to walk this path alone. Many resources and services are designed to help individuals safely leave toxic relationships. Look into local shelters and organizations specializing in domestic abuse recovery; they often provide safe housing, counseling, legal advice, and other essential services. Websites and hotlines can offer guidance and support at any hour of the day, which is invaluable when you need immediate advice or someone to talk to. These resources understand the complexities of your situation and can provide tailored advice that respects your needs and choices.

Reflection Section: Personal Safety Inventory

To further aid your preparation, take a moment to complete a personal safety inventory. Reflect on the following questions and write down your answers in a secure place:

- What are the signs that my situation is escalating?
- Who can I trust entirely to support me in this process?
- What are the safe places I can go to at short notice?
- Do I have access to all my essential personal documents, and are they stored safely?
- What local resources or organizations can assist me in this situation?

This reflection is more than an exercise; it's an act of empowering yourself with clarity and preparedness. As you fill out your inventory, remember each answer adds a layer of security and confidence to your plan, bringing you one step closer to a life of freedom and peace.

Financial Independence: Saving Yourself Economically

Gaining financial independence is like planting a garden; it starts with tiny seeds and, with consistent care, grows into something that can sustain you, offering both nourishment and a sense of accomplishment. When preparing to leave a toxic relationship, nurturing your financial independence is crucial, as it equips you with the resources to stand independently. Start by setting aside small amounts of money in a safe place where your partner cannot access it. This might mean opening a new bank account in your name only or keeping cash with a trusted friend or family member if safety is a concern. Even small contributions can grow over time, providing a financial cushion that can help cover initial expenses when you leave, such as housing, transportation, or even legal fees.

Developing an economic safety plan involves more than saving money; it includes understanding and organizing your financial assets and liabilities. Begin by gathering all essential financial documents such as bank statements, credit card statements, loan documents, and other financial obligations. Knowing the details of your financial situation is empowering and reduces the chance of surprises during your transition. It's also wise to obtain a copy of your credit report. The credit report will give you a clear picture of your credit history and alert you to any debts or issues you must be aware of. If your partner has had access to your financial information, consider changing account passwords and setting up new security measures to protect your financial data.

Seeking financial assistance is another step you can take toward economic independence. Many organizations offer financial help or advice specifically for individuals trying to leave abusive situations. Look for local nonprofits that provide grants or loans or check if there are governmental programs that offer financial support for housing, counseling, or legal aid. Online resources can also be invaluable; websites like The National Endowment for

Financial Education (NEFE) or The Financial Independence Project offer tools and articles to help you understand more about managing your finances and preparing for economic independence. Don't hesitate to contact these resources—you are not alone, and systems are in place to help you through this transition.

Building financial literacy is your final step towards economic independence. Understanding the basics of budgeting, saving, investing, and credit management can transform how you oversee money, turning it from a source of stress into a tool for empowerment. Many community centers, libraries, and nonprofits offer free or low-cost workshops on financial literacy. Online courses are also a great option, providing flexible learning opportunities that you can adapt to your schedule. Educating yourself about finances prepares you for independence. It instills more confidence in your ability to manage and direct your life post-separation.

As you work through these steps, remember that each action you take builds a foundation for your new life, one where you are free to make your own choices and free from control and manipulation. Financial independence is not just about money—it's about freedom, security, and establishing a life where your needs and well-being are prioritized. Each small step is a leap towards a future where you are economically and emotionally empowered.

Legal Considerations and Protection

Navigating the legal landscape when exiting a toxic relationship can feel like moving through a labyrinth, where each turn presents new challenges and questions. It's vital to equip yourself with knowledge about your legal rights and protections, which serve as a shield safeguarding your journey toward freedom. Understanding these legal frameworks offers protection and a profound sense of empowerment—knowing you have the law on your side can provide immense emotional support.Understanding Your Rights

The legal system, while complex, offers various protections designed to assist individuals seeking to leave abusive or toxic relationships. Familiarizing yourself with these rights can significantly impact the effectiveness of your departure strategy. Most jurisdictions have laws specifically aimed at protecting individuals from domestic abuse, which can include physical, emotional, and financial abuse. These laws typically provide:

- Mechanisms for obtaining restraining or protective orders.
- Securing temporary custody of children.
- Accessing support services such as emergency housing.

It is crucial to understand that these protections are there to serve you, irrespective of the nature of the toxicity—whether it involves physical harm or psychological manipulation. Many people hesitate to seek legal help, feeling that their situation might not be 'severe enough' to warrant it. However, the threshold for what constitutes harm is broader than most assume, and legal professionals can provide clarity and guidance.

Restraining Orders

One of the most direct forms of legal protection available is a restraining order, which legally prevents the abuser from coming into contact with you, either physically or through other means like phone calls or emails. The process for obtaining a restraining order varies by location. Still, generally, it involves filing a petition with your local court. This petition should detail the reasons you are seeking this order, including specific incidents of abuse or threats. It's essential to provide as much evidence as possible—texts, emails, witness statements, or police reports—to support your case.

Once granted, a restraining order can provide a crucial barrier, offering you space and safety. The courts take violations of restraining orders seriously, and perpetrators can face significant penalties, reinforcing the protective shield around them.

Legal Documentation

Gathering and securing necessary legal documents is another critical step in your preparation to leave. Make sure to have personal identification documents like your passport and driver's license, financial documents, marriage certificates, and any existing legal agreements or court orders. These documents are essential for filing legal forms and applications and establishing independence once you've left. Store these documents in a safe place—perhaps with a trusted friend or in a safety deposit box—to ensure they are not accessible to your partner. In cases where obtaining originals is impossible, make copies or take clear photographs. These documents are your armor, proof of your identity, and rights, which can shield you during legal proceedings.

Finding Legal Support

The prospect of engaging with the legal system can be daunting, especially when dealing with the emotional fallout of leaving a toxic relationship. However, numerous resources are available to help you navigate this process. Many legal aid societies offer services at free or reduced costs for individuals in abusive situations. These organizations can provide legal advice, help with filing paperwork, and sometimes even representation in court. Additionally, some law schools offer clinics where law students, supervised by experienced attorneys, provide legal services for free. These resources are invaluable for their direct services and the reassurance they offer—that you are not alone and that there is a structured, legal pathway out of your current situation.

As you move forward, remember that each step you take in understanding and utilizing these legal tools strengthens your position and secures your journey toward a safer life. With all its complexities, the legal system is there to protect your rights and facilitate your move away from toxicity. Engaging with it confidently, with the right resources and knowledge, can transform what might seem like a maze into a marked path to a new beginning.

Building a Support System: Finding Allies

When you find yourself on the brink of a significant life change, such as leaving a toxic relationship, the value of a robust support system cannot be stressed enough. This network, composed of individuals and groups who provide emotional solace and practical assistance, can be your anchor during turbulent times. The first critical step is identifying who can be part of this supportive circle. Look for people who have shown empathy, respect your confidentiality, and have gone through similar experiences. These individuals are likely to understand the complexities of your situation without judgment. A supportive friend, a compassionate family member, or even a trusted coworker can form the pillars of this network. Approach them honestly about your situation and the kind of support you need; this might be a safe space to stay, help with logistical arrangements, or simply a listening ear.

In addition to your connections, consider the immense benefits of joining support groups. These groups bring together individuals facing similar challenges, providing a platform for sharing experiences and strategies in a structured, supportive environment. The collective wisdom and empathy found in these groups can be incredibly empowering. Here, you'll likely find sympathy and practical advice from those who've navigated similar paths. Support groups, often facilitated by professionals, also offer guidance on coping mechanisms to help you manage stress and emotional upheaval more effectively. Whether these meetings are in-person or virtual, the sense of community and understanding they foster can significantly ease the isolation that often accompanies leaving a toxic relationship.

Leveraging online communities and forums is another strategy to broaden your support network. The digital landscape is replete with forums, social media groups, and platforms dedicated to mental health and recovery from abuse. These spaces allow you to connect with others anonymously, which can be exceptionally comforting if you're not ready to share your experiences openly. The advice and stories shared in these communities can be enlightening and uplifting. However, it's crucial to approach online interactions with discernment. Choose reputable websites and forums that are well-moderated and have a positive, supportive tone. Engage slowly by reading others' posts and progressing to sharing your own experiences as you feel more comfortable.

While building this network, maintaining your privacy and safety is paramount. Be cautious about how much personal information you share, primarily online. Use privacy settings judiciously to control who can see your posts and personal details. In face-to-face interactions, choose safe, neutral meeting places until you feel confident about your safety with new acquaintances. Remember, building a support system aims to enhance your safety and well-being, not compromise it. As you cultivate these new connections, listen to your instincts—your feelings of comfort and safety with new allies are crucial indicators of whether a relationship will be supportive.

Navigating the process of building a support system while planning significant life changes is undoubtedly challenging. Still, with careful thought and strategic choices, this network can provide tremendous strength and reassurance. As you move forward, each positive interaction and supportive relationship adds a layer of security and confidence, reinforcing your resolve and ability to transition into a new phase of life with robust backing.

Setting Boundaries: The First Step to

Boundaries are the invisible lines we draw around ourselves to protect our peace and personal dignity. They are the unwritten rules that signal to others how they can treat us, what is acceptable, and what is not. In the context of leaving a toxic relationship, setting clear boundaries is not just a beneficial tool; it is a crucial strategy for safeguarding your mental health and physical well-being. Boundaries help you to define yourself in terms of who you are, what you believe, and how you will engage with others, making them essential during times of significant change. When these boundaries are respected, they create a sense of stability and security. However, when boundaries are ignored, it can lead to feelings of violation and disrespect, which is often the case in toxic relationships.

Consider setting several types of boundaries: physical, emotional, and digital. Physical boundaries relate to your personal space and physical touch. You should know how you interact with people who come into your home. Emotional boundaries protect your psychological well-being by controlling who can access your emotions and under what circumstances you engage emotionally. That includes deciding not to discuss certain topics with specific people if such conversations leave you drained or upset. Digital boundaries, meanwhile, pertain to how you interact with technology and how others can interact with you through digital channels. You may decide to set boundaries by having rules about accepting or not accepting friend requests from coworkers or setting your social media profiles to private.

Communicating your boundaries clearly and effectively is vital. Begin by being as specific as possible about your boundaries and why they are essential to you. Use "I" statements to express your needs, such as "I need some time alone each evening to recharge," rather than phrases that can be perceived as accusatory, like "You're always bothering me." Be calm and assertive when communicating your boundaries. Remember, setting boundaries is not an act of aggression; it's an act of self-respect. If you feel nervous, practice what you want to say beforehand. Discussing these boundaries during a neutral time, not in the heat of an argument, can also be helpful to ensure that you are communicating clearly.

Enforcing these boundaries can often be more challenging than setting them, primarily if others are used to you having none. Stay consistent and firm when people are testing your boundaries. For example, if you've asked not to be called after 9 PM but someone keeps calling, do not answer the phone. If the person brings it up later, restate your boundary calmly and firmly. It's essential to act according to your boundaries, not just communicate them. Sometimes, you must enforce these boundaries by removing yourself from situations or relationships that continuously disrespect your limits. For instance, if a friend repeatedly violates your emotional boundaries by dismissing your feelings, stepping back from that friendship might be necessary.

Remember, setting and maintaining boundaries is a skill that requires practice and dedication. Initially, you might feel guilty or selfish, especially if you are not used to prioritizing your needs. However, firm boundaries are a sign of self-respect and self-care. They don't just protect you; they also teach others how to treat you, creating healthier dynamics in your relationships. As you navigate this process, give yourself grace. Adjusting to these changes takes time, and it's okay to reassess your boundaries as your situation and feelings evolve. Each step in enforcing your boundaries reaffirms your right to a respectful and fulfilling life.

The Role of Technology in Escaping Toxicity

In our digital era, technology plays a crucial role in almost every aspect of our lives, and its influence extends into how we manage personal safety and privacy, particularly when planning to leave a toxic relationship. Securing your online presence is essential to safeguarding your journey to freedom. Take deliberate actions to protect your online accounts and personal information, which, if accessed by an abuser, could jeopardize your safety and privacy. Start by changing passwords on all your important accounts—email, bank accounts, social media, and other platforms containing personal information. Choose firm, unique passwords for each account to prevent the abuser from gaining access through shared or similar passwords. Additionally, enable two-factor authentication wherever possible. An extra layer of security ensures that accessing your accounts requires more than just the password.

The realm of digital interaction also presents opportunities for abusers to misuse technology to stalk or control. GPS tracking, spyware, and unauthorized access to your devices are common tactics used by abusers to maintain control over their victims. It's essential to regularly check your devices for any signs of unauthorized access or tracking apps. Consider consulting a professional to examine your devices if you suspect they might be compromised. Furthermore, limit the use of shared devices or accounts that could give your abuser insight into your plans or whereabouts. Being mindful of the apps you use and understanding the permissions you grant them can also prevent inadvertent sharing of your location or other sensitive information.

While the risks are significant, technology also offers powerful tools you can use to escape a toxic relationship. Use your smartphone or computer to gather and store evidence of abuse, which can be helpful in legal proceedings or securing restraining orders. Consider saving texts, emails, voicemails, and even recording threatening or abusive interactions, provided it's legal in your area. Cloud storage services can be beneficial for backing up important documents and evidence safely where the abuser cannot physically destroy or tamper with them. Additionally, technology provides access to many resources and support networks online. From apps designed to help victims of domestic abuse to forums and social media groups offering support and advice, the digital world is full of resources that can help you feel less isolated and more empowered as you plan your exit.

Managing your privacy settings across all platforms is another crucial step in using technology safely. Ensure that your social media accounts are set to private and review your friend lists to remove or block the abuser and their associates. Be cautious about sharing information online that could reveal your location or new contact details. Regularly review the privacy settings on all platforms to ensure they align with your current needs for safety and privacy. Additionally, be aware of your digital footprint—the trail of data you leave behind as you use the internet. Think about social media, public records, and other online activities. Minimizing your digital footprint can reduce the risk of your abuser tracking your activities and location, contributing to your overall safety as you transition away from the relationship.

As we wrap up this chapter on preparing to leave, it's clear that the journey to safety is multi-faceted, involving careful planning and strategic use of available resources. From securing your finances and legal rights to leveraging technology and building a supportive network, each step empowers you with the tools you need to exit a toxic relationship safely. As you move forward, remember that these preparations are not just practical measures but affirmations of your right to live a life free from abuse and control. In the next chapter, we will explore the actual process of leaving, providing guidance on navigating this critical transition smoothly and safely.

Break the Silence

You don't let go of a bad relationship because you stop caring about them. You let go because you start caring about yourself.

Charles Orlando

When you are in a toxic relationship, so much of your attention gets caught up in what you consider wrong, unacceptable, or downright abusive in your partner's behavior. Distancing yourself from the pain for a while to see how you arrived at the precise point of life you're at, however, is one of the most challenging yet rewarding parts of leaving a life of toxicity behind.

It is never about self-blame but rather, about self-knowledge. Without knowing your own attachment and conflict styles and without connecting past traumas with current toxic bonds, you may end one toxic relationship only to embark on another. Throughout the pages of this book, I have stressed that we are all the products of the patterns we observed and absorbed in our childhood. If there is one positive to take from being in a toxic relationship, it is that we can decide to break free from the past and embrace relationships characterized by love, respect, and mutual caring. And the only person you can change is yourself. If you find that this book is enlightening you on your thoughts, emotions, and behaviors, and showing you how to make healthy changes, please share your opinion with others.

By leaving a review of this book on Amazon, you'll show new readers that the way out of a toxic relationship begins with greater self-awareness.

Simply by leaving a sentence or two and a little bit about your own story (if you wish), you can help someone escape the trap of inertia to pursue a happier and more meaningful life.

Thanks for your support. May your courage and strength move you away from toxicity and toward healthy, mutually satisfying relationships.

Scan the QR code below:

5

The Act of Leaving

A s you contemplate leaving a toxic relationship, you may experience a blend of daunting uncertainty and invigorating possibility. The act of leaving—physically stepping into a new chapter—can evoke a complex tapestry of emotions and logistical challenges. Here, we delve into the practical and emotional preparations essential for a safe and empowered departure. This journey, while challenging, marks a profound act of self-respect and courage, affirming your right to a healthier, happier existence.

The Logistics of Leaving: What to Expect

Planning Your Exit: Step-by-step Guidance

Mapping out your departure is like setting the coordinates for a destination you deserve—a life free of toxicity. Start by choosing a day and time when your partner is least likely to be home, reducing the risk of confrontation. This might be during their regular work hours or a known appointment. Prepare a checklist of essential items to take with you, focusing on necessities such as important documents (identification, financial records, legal papers), clothing for a few days, essential medications, and valuable personal items that hold emotional significance or practical utility.

Consider the logistical aspects of your exit as well. Plan your transportation in advance—whether arranging a ride with a friend, booking a taxi, or locating your nearest public transport facilities. If you are taking your vehicle, ensure it is fueled and functions well ahead of time. Additionally, ensure your phone is fully charged, and you have a charger with you; maintaining communication lines during and after your departure is crucial for logistic coordination and emotional support.

Finding a Safe Place: Options for Shelter

Securing a safe destination is your next crucial step. If staying with friends or family, confirm arrangements with them in advance, ensuring they understand the need for confidentiality and security. For many, local shelters provide an anonymous and secure option. These facilities are equipped to help individuals fleeing from abusive situations and often offer additional support services such as counseling and legal aid. Research and contact these shelters ahead of time to understand their availability and any required procedures. Remember, the aim is to move towards a space that guarantees your safety and offers an environment where you can begin healing.

Immediate Legal Considerations

Legal preparations can fortify your departure with an additional layer of protection. If you believe there's a risk of immediate harm upon departure, consider filing for a restraining order. Contact a local domestic violence agency or seek legal counsel to understand the specifics of obtaining such an order in your area. This legal barrier can significantly deter the abuser from attempting contact and provide you with legal recourse if they do. Also, inform yourself about the legal considerations relevant to your situation, such as rights to shared assets, custody of children, or obligations from shared financial agreements. Knowledge of these factors is crucial and can influence decisions in your initial steps after leaving.

Self-Care During Departure

Amid the whirlwind of logistical preparations, nurturing your emotional and physical well-being is paramount. The stress of leaving a toxic relationship can take a significant toll on your health. Prioritize self-care practices that maintain your strength and clarity. Include simple routines like eating regular, nutritious meals and staying hydrated throughout the departure process. Use brief exercises or breathing techniques to manage stress and help maintain a calm mind. Rest and lean on supportive friends or counselors to share your feelings and fears. Self-care is not an indulgence but an essential part of maintaining your resilience and focus during this critical time.

In this chapter, as you navigate the complexities of leaving a toxic relationship, remember that each step you take is a testament to your strength and commitment to a better life. While the road may seem fraught with challenges, each task you undertake paves the way to freedom and healing. The strategies and preparations discussed are not just plans; they affirm your worth and right to a safe and fulfilling life. As you proceed, carry with you the courage and hope that have brought you to this point, and trust that each step forward is a step towards a new beginning.

Handling Confrontation: Strategies for the Moment of Departure

In the delicate moments of leaving a toxic relationship, managing the potential for confrontation is crucial for ensuring both your safety and emotional well-being. It's about navigating this critical transition with as much grace and calm as you can muster, equipped with strategies that help you maintain control over the situation. Often, the goal is to leave without sparking conflict, a tactical move that involves careful timing and preparation. Choosing a moment when the person you are going to is not present is ideal; perhaps they are at work or out on a routine errand. This timing minimally disrupts emotions and reduces the chances of a confrontation. If this isn't possible, another method is to have a trusted friend or family member present, which can help control the situation and provide you with emotional support.

However, even with the best-laid plans, confrontations might arise, and knowing how to de-escalate these situations is essential. De-escalation techniques are like verbal judo; they're about deflecting and calming rather than meeting aggression with more aggression. Your tone of voice, calm and even, can be a powerful tool to soothe tensions. Use affirming, non-confrontational language and avoid accusatory statements. Phrases like "I understand your feelings" or "Let's discuss this calmly" can help alleviate a heated moment. It's also helpful to keep your statements focused on your feelings and needs rather than the other person's faults. For instance, saying, "I need to feel safe and respected," centers the conversation around your needs without directly blaming the other person, which can sometimes prevent escalation.

In some cases, involving authorities is necessary to protect your safety. If you anticipate that leaving might put you at immediate risk of harm, having a plan for involving the police is critical. You might arrange for law enforcement to be present during your departure, especially in cases where previous threats or acts of violence have occurred. The presence of law enforcement can act as a deterrent against violent actions. It can provide you with a sense of security as you leave. Knowing the non-emergency numbers for your local police station or discussing your situation with them in advance can prepare them to respond more swiftly and effectively if needed.

Preparing emotionally for the reactions—both yours and theirs—is equally important. Leaving a toxic relationship can be an emotional rollercoaster fraught with guilt, fear, relief, and uncertainty. Prioritize self-compassion during this time. Recognize that feeling a complex array of emotions is normal and allow yourself space to feel these emotions without judgment. Practicing mindfulness techniques, such as deep breathing or meditation, can help manage anxiety and maintain emotional equilibrium. Remember, this moment is about setting a new course for your life that leads to healthier, safer places. By approaching this departure with preparedness and calm, you equip yourself with the best tools to navigate this challenging yet transformative phase of your life.

Protecting Children During the Separation

When the decision to leave a toxic relationship involves children, the dynamics become significantly more delicate. The little ones, often silent bearers of the emotional burden, need special consideration to ensure their safety and emotional stability during this tumultuous period. Prioritizing children's safety involves a multi-faceted approach, starting with securing a safe environment. As you plan your exit, consider immediate and temporary accommodations that are child-friendly and secure. You may need to arrange stays with family members who have a nurturing relationship with your children or secure spots in specialized shelters that accommodate mothers with children. Ensure that these places are safe from physical harm and provide a stable environment to minimize disruption to your children's daily routines, such as school and recreational activities.

On the emotional front, children need clear and appropriate communication about the changes in their lives. Depending on their age and maturity level, explain the situation in a way they can understand without overwhelming them with adult problems or graphic details. It's crucial to reassure them that they are not at fault, that both parents love them, and that everyone's safety and happiness are the priority. Frame the discussion around the positives of the new arrangements, such as being in a happier, calmer environment. Validate any feelings they express and be ready to support them through feelings of confusion, sadness, or anger. Consider discussing counseling at this time. A professional can help them articulate and deal with their emotions constructively.

Legal considerations regarding custody during this period are paramount. Begin by consulting with a legal professional who specializes in family law. Understand your rights and responsibilities under the law concerning child custody and support. If you anticipate custody disputes, prepare by documenting your evidence for the compromise of the child's welfare under the other parent's care. This documentation can be prioritized in legal settings when the courts consider decisions about the child's primary residence and visitation rights. Also, inform your children's schools and caretakers about the situation in appropriate terms to ensure they are not inadvertently released to the other parent if there are safety concerns. Schools and daycare centers can be allies in maintaining your children's safety during transitions.

To further support children affected by toxic relationships, numerous resources can provide guidance and comfort. Look for books and age-appropriate materials dealing with change themes, family challenges, and emotional resilience. Organizations such as the National Child Traumatic Stress Network offer resources specifically designed to help children navigate the emotional effects of toxic relationships in the family. If needed, engage with local child psychologists or child welfare organizations that can provide professional assessments and interventions. These resources can offer immediate support and long-term strategies to help your children heal and adapt to new life circumstances.

Navigating a separation with children in the context of a toxic relationship requires careful consideration of their physical safety and emotional health. By creating a secure environment, maintaining open and supportive communication, addressing legal necessities, and utilizing available resources, you can safeguard their well-being during this critical transition. This approach helps mitigate the impact of the current changes. It lays the groundwork for their future resilience and emotional health. Remember, the steps you take now are crucial in shaping their perception of safety and security in relationships as they grow.

Managing Mutual Friends and Social Circles

Navigating the intricate web of mutual friendships and social circles post-departure can be a delicate endeavor, ripe with potential for emotional strain and opportunities for support and new beginnings. When you step away from a toxic relationship, the ripple effects can extend into your broader social network, stirring up a range of dynamics that require careful handling. This phase involves tact and thoughtfulness, as the reactions of mutual friends can significantly influence your emotional landscape during this transition.

When deciding how to communicate your departure to mutual friends and acquaintances, consider the level of information necessary and appropriate for different circles. It's vital to balance maintaining your privacy and being open enough to receive support. In cases where friends are closely connected to you and your former partner, keep the information factual and neutral. You might say, "I wanted you to hear from me that [Name] and I have decided to go our separate ways. I appreciate your support during this time." This approach respects your boundaries and those of your listeners, preventing the spread of speculation and taking control of your narrative.

Handling loyalty conflicts among mutual friends can be one of the more challenging aspects of your social transition. It's common for friends to feel caught in the middle, trying to figure out how to support both parties without appearing to take sides. Be prepared for some friends to choose allegiances based on their perspectives or pre-existing relationships. While this can be painful, approach these situations with understanding and grace. Recognize that their relationship history and emotional capacities shape each person's reaction. If a friend struggles with maintaining neutrality, consider having a one-on-one discussion to express your feelings and needs directly. Explain that you value their support and friendship and clarify how they can help you feel supported. Ask your friend not to share information about you with your ex-partner or express your need for positive interactions that don't involve discussing the breakup.

Building a new supportive community post-departure is necessary for emotional recovery and growth. Start by identifying environments and activities that align with your interests and values. Joining clubs, groups, or classes can be excellent ways to meet new people while engaging in activities that boost your mood and self-esteem. Look for local community events or volunteering opportunities where you can connect with people in a structured and positive setting. Online platforms can also be valuable for finding local meetups or groups that share your hobbies or support needs. As you build this new network, focus on fostering connections with individuals who demonstrate empathy, respect, and positivity. These relationships will form the cornerstone of your latest social circle, providing a foundation of support and joy in your post-toxic relationship life.

Navigating the changes in your social circles after leaving a toxic relationship requires patience and self-compassion. It's a process that might test your emotional resilience but also offers a unique opportunity to reshape your social world in ways that affirm your values and nurture your well-being. Communicating thoughtfully, handling conflicts with understanding, and actively seeking out positive new connections set the stage for a social environment supporting your healing and growth. As you move forward, remember that each interaction is a step toward a community that respects and enriches your life, reflecting the new beginnings you deserve.

The Immediate Aftermath: Navigating the First Few Days

The initial days following your departure from a toxic relationship often unfold like an intense storm of emotions. As the adrenaline of leaving wanes, you may find yourself on an emotional rollercoaster, feeling waves of relief, fear, sadness, and even doubt about your decision. Acknowledging and preparing for this emotional upheaval as a natural response to the significant change you've just initiated in your life is vital. These feelings are valid and expected; they do not signify weakness or regret but are part of the healing process. Allowing yourself to feel these emotions without judgment is essential during this time. Engage in quiet reflection or journaling to process what you're going through. These activities can help you acknowledge your feelings, understand them, and gradually gain control over them. Remember, these emotions are transient—they will ebb and flow and eventually stabilize as you adjust to your new circumstances.

In parallel with managing your emotional health, practical steps need immediate attention to ensure your ongoing safety and stability. First, secure your accommodation temporarily at a shelter, a friend's house, or a new apartment. Ensure your new living situation is safe and you have the essentials for a few days, such as food, basic household supplies, and personal items. Next, take steps to secure your financial independence. Consider opening a new bank account, redirecting your mail, and updating your billing information for essentials like your phone and utilities. If you still need to do so, change passwords and security settings on your digital devices and online accounts to ensure your privacy and security further.

Additionally, it's crucial to consider the legal steps you may need to take immediately. If you haven't filed for a restraining order and your situation warrants it, now might be the time to do so. Consult a legal advisor to understand your rights and the necessary actions to protect yourself. Make sure to include securing assets, starting divorce proceedings, or other legal separations. Each of these steps, while possibly daunting, is about putting building blocks in place for your new life, ensuring that you are legally and financially buffered against further manipulation or abuse.

During such a transformative phase, prioritizing self-care is crucial. The stress of what you're going through can take a significant toll on both your physical and mental health. Develop a self-care routine that includes activities that nourish and rejuvenate you. You might take a daily walk to clear your mind, practice meditation or yoga, or engage in a hobby you love but have to set aside during your relationship. Ensure you eat well-balanced meals and get enough sleep, as physical health significantly impacts emotional resilience. Most importantly, allow yourself moments of peace to breathe and be, affirming your right to rest and personal space, which you or your partner might have compromised in your past relationship.

Lastly, seeking professional help during this period can be immensely beneficial. This help can come in various forms—counseling to help you deal with the emotional aftermath, legal advice to navigate separations and protective orders, or financial advice to regain control over your economic situation. Professionals can provide expert advice and emotional support, helping you feel less alone and more empowered to manage the challenges you face. Do not hesitate to seek out support groups where you can share your experiences and learn from others who have been in similar situations. These groups can offer practical advice, emotional support, and an invaluable sense of community during such a vulnerable time.

Embracing this support, acknowledging your emotions without judgment, and taking practical steps to secure your immediate needs are all part of navigating the aftermath of leaving a toxic relationship. Each action reinforces your decision to choose a healthier, safer life, steadily moving from surviving to thriving in your new reality. As you move forward, remember that each day brings you further from your past and closer to a future filled with hope and new possibilities.

Dealing with Hoovering and Other Tactics to Lure You Back

In the aftermath of leaving a toxic relationship, you might find yourself facing a series of manipulative tactics designed to pull you back into the turmoil you just escaped. Understanding these tactics, particularly hoovering, is critical as they often affect your vulnerabilities and emotions, making you question your decision to leave. Hoovering, named after the famous vacuum cleaner brand, involves the abuser attempting to "suck" you back into the relationship through various manipulative strategies. These can range from seemingly heartfelt apologies and promises to change to gifts, romantic gestures, or shared memories meant to evoke nostalgia and doubt in your decision.

Recognizing these tactics is your first line of defense. Aside from hoovering, abusers might employ guilt trips, where they portray themselves as the victim of circumstances or your departure, claiming they cannot cope without you. There might be dramatic displays of affection or public declarations of love, especially on social media, designed to pull at your heartstrings and create public pressure to return. Another common tactic is using mutual friends or even children as messengers or tools to convey sentiments of regret and loneliness, hoping to trigger your empathy and responsibility to mend the relationship. These actions are manipulative strategies that aim not to address the issues that led to your departure but to regain control over you.

Staying firm in your decision to leave requires emotional resilience and practical strategies. Begin by reaffirming your reasons for leaving—write them down if you have to and revisit them whenever you feel uncertain. Engage in activities and hobbies that strengthen your sense of self and independence, reinforcing the benefits of your new life free from manipulation. It's also helpful to set strict no-contact rules or at least limited contact if co-parenting demands some interaction. Change your phone number, if necessary, block them on social media, and set clear boundaries with mutual friends regarding what information you are comfortable sharing.

Seeking support plays an indispensable role in maintaining your resolve. Surround yourself with friends and family who understand your situation and support your decision to leave. Sometimes, discussing the manipulative tactics with someone with your best interests at heart can help you see them for what they are —desperate attempts to regain control. Furthermore, professional help from a counselor or therapist skilled in dealing with abusive relationships can provide you with additional coping strategies. These professionals can help you understand the psychological underpinnings of your ex-partner's behavior and offer practical advice on staying detached and safe.

Navigating this minefield of manipulation post-departure is no small feat. It demands strength, clarity, and a solid support system. By understanding and recognizing the tactics used to lure you back, staying firm in your resolve, and leaning on the support of loved ones and professionals, you fortify your boundaries and affirm your commitment to a healthier, happier life. Remember, each day away from the toxic relationship helps you reclaim your autonomy and rebuild a life founded on respect and genuine affection, not manipulation and control.

Ending Reflection

As we close this chapter, let's reflect on the critical insights and strategies discussed. Dealing with hoovering and other manipulative tactics is about recognizing these maneuvers for what they are—desperate attempts to entangle you in the toxicity you worked so hard to escape. Your firmness in maintaining the boundaries you've set, bolstered by the support of friends, family, and professionals, is essential in this phase of your healing journey. These steps are about avoiding regression and progressing towards a life that celebrates and respects your independence and well-being. As we turn the page to the next chapter, we carry forward the strength and wisdom gained here, ready to face new challenges and embrace life's opportunities free from toxicity.

6

Post-Escape Challenges

As the dust settles on the roads once traveled, you find yourself at a new dawn, the immediate fears of escape behind you. Yet, this fresh horizon brings its own set of challenges and emotional landscapes to navigate. Stepping into this new phase of your life, you might notice the scars left by your past experiences, not just as reminders of what you've endured but as beacons guiding your path to healing and self-reclamation. This chapter is dedicated to understanding and navigating the emotional aftermath of leaving a toxic relationship—a journey back to yourself and the person you aspire to become.

Emotional Turmoil: Healing from Psychological Scars

Understanding the Healing Process

Emerging from a toxic relationship, you may feel like someone recovering from a long illness, slowly regaining strength, and learning to function again in the everyday world. The emotional healing process is complex and multifaceted, involving stages of grief, anger, confusion, and reconstruction of your self-identity. Just as the body takes time to heal from physical wounds, your psyche needs time to recover from the emotional wounds inflicted by toxicity. Recognizing this process as a natural response to the significant changes and traumas you've experienced is vital. Healing is not linear—some days will feel like a leap forward, while others might seem like a step back. Each phase, however painful or slow, is a pivotal part of the recovery journey, helping you process your experiences and eventually find closure.

Identifying and Addressing Trauma

Trauma, often a byproduct of toxic relationships, can manifest in various forms, including anxiety, flashbacks, nightmares, or overwhelming feelings of sadness or anger. Recognizing these symptoms as signs of trauma is the first step in addressing them. It's crucial to validate your feelings and understand that they are normal reactions to abnormal experiences. Seeking therapy from a professional who specializes in trauma and abuse can provide you with the tools to work through these emotions in a safe and structured environment. Therapies like Cognitive Behavioral Therapy (CBT) or Eye Movement Desensitization and Reprocessing (EMDR) have proven effective in helping individuals process and overcome trauma. These therapeutic approaches can help you reframe your experiences and regain control over your emotional responses, facilitating a more profound healing process.

Coping Mechanisms

Developing healthy coping mechanisms is essential in managing the symptoms of trauma and facilitating emotional healing. Techniques such as mindfulness meditation, deep breathing exercises, and progressive muscle relaxation can significantly reduce symptoms of anxiety and stress. Engaging in regular physical activity can also be incredibly beneficial; exercise not only helps to release endorphins (natural mood lifters) but also helps to break the cycle of negative thoughts that often accompany depression. Additionally, creative outlets like writing, painting, or music provide expressive ways to process complex emotions and can be incredibly therapeutic. It's important to explore different coping strategies and find the ones that work best for you, providing comfort and stability as you navigate your healing journey.

Patience with Self

Above all, healing from the emotional scars of a toxic relationship requires patience and self-compassion. The process can be painfully slow, and it's easy to become frustrated with your perceived lack of progress. Remember, you cannot rush healing. It's important to treat yourself with the same kindness and understanding during this time as you would a good friend. Celebrate small victories, acknowledge your growth, and be gentle with yourself on more challenging days. Self-compassion isn't just about being kind to yourself in the moment—it's about building a nurturing relationship with yourself that can sustain you through this journey.

Reflective Journaling Exercise: Mapping Your Emotional Landscape

Engaging in this reflective journaling exercise will further aid your understanding and navigation of the emotional healing process. Take a moment to write about your current emotional state, noting any feelings or symptoms you experience frequently. Reflect on how you tie these emotions to your past relationship. Then, brainstorm coping strategies you found helpful or would like to try.

This exercise can help you visualize your emotional landscape and path to managing and overcoming these feelings, reinforcing your agency in your healing process.

Co-parenting with a Toxic Ex: Strategies for Sanity

Navigating the complexities of co-parenting with a toxic ex-partner requires a delicate balance of firm boundaries, legal knowledge, emotional management, and support systems. While daunting, this task is crucial not only for your well-being but also for your children's emotional and psychological health. Establishing and maintaining clear boundaries in your co-parenting arrangements lays the groundwork for a structured, less stressful relationship with your ex-partner. It's essential to define what is acceptable and what isn't in terms of interactions, responsibilities, and communication. For instance, deciding that all communication should be written (like texts or emails) can help keep exchanges brief, focused, and devoid of emotional charge. Doing this also provides a documented trail of interactions, which can be invaluable in disputes. Additionally, setting boundaries around your availability—specifying days and times when you can discuss co-parenting matters—helps manage your ex-partner's access to you, thereby reducing opportunities for manipulation or unwanted intrusion into your personal life.

Legal protection and rights play a pivotal role in safeguarding your and your children's interests. Familiarizing yourself with your legal rights regarding custody and co-parenting is essential. You may have to consult a family law attorney who can provide guidance tailored to your situation. Understanding and utilizing legal measures such as custody agreements that specify scheduling, visitation rights, and decision-making authorities can provide a structured framework that minimizes conflict. In some cases, where there is a history of abuse or manipulation, legal stipulations can also include supervised visitations or mandatory counseling for the toxic ex-partner as conditions for visitation rights. These legal instruments are not just formalities; they are tools that protect your children's well-being and your peace of mind.

Maintaining emotional distance while co-parenting with a toxic ex is crucial for your mental health and for setting a healthy example for your children. You must recognize and resist any hooks that your ex might use to draw you into old patterns of conflict or manipulation. Techniques such as disengaging from unnecessary confrontations, avoiding personal discussions beyond the necessary co-parenting interactions, and focusing on objective communication about the children's needs can help maintain this distance. It can be helpful to visualize your interactions as business-like, where the "business" is the well-being and upbringing of your children. This mindset can help you stay focused on important things and avoid getting drawn into emotional turmoil.

Building a robust support system is invaluable in navigating the challenges of co-parenting with a toxic ex. This system should include close friends and family who can offer emotional support and practical help and professionals like therapists or counselors who can provide guidance and coping strategies. Parenting groups —both online and in-person—can also be a great resource, offering camaraderie and shared experiences from those in similar situations. These groups can provide support, practical advice, and strategies that have worked for others in similar circumstances. Additionally, consider seeking out workshops or classes on effective co-parenting; these can provide you with tools and techniques to manage the challenges of co-parenting with a toxic ex, helping you to maintain your sanity and focus on raising healthy, happy children.

In your journey to manage co-parenting challenges, remember that the goal is to create a stable and nurturing environment for your children despite the complexities of dealing with a toxic ex. You can navigate this challenging aspect of post-separation life with greater confidence and peace by setting clear boundaries, utilizing legal protections, maintaining emotional distance, and leaning on a solid support system.

Rebuilding Your Life: First Steps Towards a New Beginning

After stepping away from the shadows of a toxic relationship, you find yourself at the threshold of an expansive and bright new phase of your life. It's a time filled with potential, a blank canvas upon which you can redefine who you are and what you truly desire from life. Rediscovering yourself might seem daunting at first—like getting reacquainted with an old friend you haven't seen in years. Begin by exploring your interests, those things you once loved but perhaps set aside or lost in the tumult of your past relationship. Maybe it was painting, hiking, reading, or something as simple as spending quiet mornings in a café. Allow yourself to revisit these passions without pressure or expectation. Engage with them as avenues of exploration and joy, not as tasks to be mastered.

As you reconnect with these activities, remember how they make you feel. Do they bring a sense of peace? Excitement? Nostalgia? This emotional feedback is a powerful guide, helping you understand where your true interests lie and what you might have suppressed in your past toxic environment. Engaging in these rediscovered passions is also a profound statement of your independence—it's you choosing to do something purely for yourself, asserting your preferences and desires in a world that is once again yours to shape.

Establishing an independent post-toxic relationship is crucial, not just emotionally but also practically. Start with the basics, like finding a job or securing housing if you still need to do so. These steps can seem overwhelming, so break them down into manageable tasks. For job hunting, begin by updating your resume or LinkedIn profile. Contact your network or consider joining professional groups to meet new contacts and learn about opportunities. When finding a place to live, consider what environment best supports healing and growth. The best environment might be a quiet neighborhood, a bustling city center close to friends, or a new town. As you establish these foundations, you are not just building a life free from toxicity but creating a sanctuary that reflects and supports who you are and all you are becoming.

Building a new support network is another essential step in this phase of your life. Start by contacting old friends or making new ones in classes, workshops, or community events that align with your interests. When forming new friendships, focus on people who uplift and support you, those who respect your boundaries and encourage your growth. If you're open to it, consider dating again, but do so from the standpoint of curiosity and self-respect, clear about your boundaries and the attributes you value in a partner. Remember, this new network of friends and potential partners isn't just about socializing—it's about constructing a community that mirrors the values and respect you hold dear.

Setting goals for the future is both a practical and motivational process that can guide your continued growth and ensure that your new life aligns with your values and aspirations. Start with short-term goals, like completing a course or organizing your new home, which can provide immediate satisfaction and a sense of accomplishment. Then, consider your long-term goals. These include career advancements, education, travel, or personal projects like writing a book or starting a business. Setting these goals gives you direction and purpose, something to strive towards. It also serves as a reminder of your agency in your life—the power you have to shape your future according to your desires and dreams.

As you take these steps towards rebuilding your life, remember that each choice you make, each boundary you set, and each goal you pursue reflects your growing strength and independence. This reconstruction period is about more than just recovery; it's about moving forward into an authentically yours-filled life filled with passion, peace, and possibilities. Embrace this time with patience and optimism and allow yourself to enjoy the process of discovering who you are now and all that you can be.

The Legal Battle: Navigating Custody and Restraining Orders

Navigating the legal landscape after leaving a toxic relationship can often feel like you are stepping into a bewildering world filled with unfamiliar terms and daunting procedures, especially when it involves custody battles and restraining orders. Understanding this process is crucial for your peace of mind and securing your future and that of your children. The legal process for these matters typically begins with filing petitions or applications. In the case of custody, you will need to file for custody in the family court, and the process may involve several hearings where both parties present their case. For restraining orders, the process often requires you to demonstrate immediate danger or ongoing harassment, necessitating legal protection. In both scenarios, the court's decision aims to prioritize safety and well-being, focusing on what is best for the children in custody cases.

Preparation for your court appearances is critical. Start by gathering all relevant evidence that supports your case. Make sure to include text messages, emails, witness statements, or any documentation that proves harassment, abuse, or an unstable living environment created by your ex-partner. Maintaining a detailed log of interactions with your ex-partner is also beneficial, especially if they pertain to breaches of existing orders or agreements. Understanding legal terminology and the implications of various legal decisions can significantly impact the outcomes of your case. Familiarize yourself with terms like 'sole custody,' 'joint custody,' 'visitation rights,' 'restraining order,' and 'protective order.' These terms determine the nature of legal arrangements and their impact on your life post-trial.

When seeking legal aid, it's essential to find a lawyer who specializes in family law or domestic violence cases. They can provide you with the expertise needed to navigate the complexities of the legal system effectively. If financial constraints pose a challenge, seek legal aid services offered by non-profit organizations or pro bono services where lawyers provide free legal assistance. Many domestic violence shelters and agencies have connections with legal professionals who are particularly sensitive to the needs of those escaping abusive situations. These professionals guide you through the legal process and understand the emotional nuances that accompany these cases.

The emotional toll of legal battles, particularly those involving custody and restraining orders, cannot be underestimated. During this challenging time, emotional support is paramount. Lean on close friends and family for support—those who can offer a listening ear and practical help, such as accompanying you to court or helping with childcare during legal appointments. Engaging with a therapist or counselor who specializes in post-traumatic stress and family law can help you manage the emotional strain associated with these proceedings. Support groups for single parents or survivors of domestic abuse can also offer comfort and advice, connecting you with others who have navigated similar challenges. These groups often provide a sense of community and understanding that is incredibly reassuring during such a tumultuous period.

Navigating custody battles and restraining orders is a complex process that requires legal knowledge, careful preparation, and robust emotional support. Understanding each step of the legal process, preparing thoroughly for court, seeking specialized legal aid, and surrounding yourself with a strong support network will equip you with the tools necessary to navigate these challenges effectively. This approach helps you manage the stress and demands of legal battles and lays the groundwork for a safer, more stable future for yourself and your children. As you move forward, remember that each step taken in this legal journey is a step towards reclaiming your autonomy and safeguarding your well-being and that of your loved ones.

Financial Recovery After Toxic Relationships

Stepping out of the shadows of a toxic relationship often means reevaluating and rebuilding many aspects of your life, including your finances, which may have taken a hit. The process of financial recovery is much like tending to a garden that has been left unattended; it requires time, patience, and a bit of strategy to bring it back to health. Let's first address how to gauge the financial impact and begin setting the stage for a robust economic recovery.

Assessing the financial damage is the initial step. You must take a comprehensive inventory of all your financial accounts, including checking, savings, credit cards, loans, and investments. Look at your balances, the terms of your debts, and any outstanding obligations. It's also crucial to pull your credit report, which will give you a clear picture of all your liabilities and how lenders view your financial health. This report can reveal any discrepancies or unexpected debts you were unaware of, which is common in situations where another party manipulated or mishandled finances. Organizing this information allows you to see the full scope of your financial situation, which is the first step towards regaining control.

Creating a budget is your following tool for empowerment. With a clear understanding of your income and expenditures, you can allocate funds to essential expenses, such as housing, food, utilities, and transportation. Be sure to include minimum debt payments to avoid penalties and further damage to your credit score. This might also be the time to identify areas where you can cut back, such as subscription services or non-essential spending, to free up more savings and debt repayment funds. Budgeting apps or tools can be beneficial in tracking your expenses and staying on target. The budget you create isn't just a financial document; it reflects your priorities and a blueprint for achieving your financial independence.

Building financial health is the next phase, shifting focus from stabilization to growth. Start with addressing any immediate credit issues. If you have outstanding debts, contact your creditors to discuss your situation. Many companies have hardship programs that allow you to lower your interest rates or reduce monthly payments. Once you've stabilized your debts, focus on rebuilding your credit. Consistent, timely payments are vital to improving your credit score.

Additionally, consider adding new forms of credit, like a secured credit card, which can help boost your score if you manage them responsibly. As your finances stabilize, start setting aside a portion of your income into a savings account. This fund is a financial cushion, reducing stress and providing security for future uncertainties.

Lastly, it would help if you viewed financial independence as a form of empowerment. Each step to repair and build your financial health reinforces your autonomy and freedom from past constraints. It's not just about money; it's about having the freedom to make life choices that align with your values and goals. Financial independence means less stress and more options, whether pursuing a new career, furthering your education, traveling, or investing in your future. Embrace this process as an integral part of building a new life where you are in control, where each financial decision you make is a building block in a foundation of self-sufficiency and resilience.

By meticulously assessing your financial damage, creating a thoughtful budget, actively rebuilding your financial health, and viewing financial independence as a critical component of your empowerment, you are not just recovering but thriving. These steps are about reclaiming what was lost and forging ahead to a future where financial stability supports your life's dreams and ambitions.

Finding and Creating Safe Spaces for Healing

The environments we inhabit—both physically and emotionally—play a pivotal role in our healing processes. As you move beyond a toxic relationship, finding and creating safe spaces where you can feel secure, comfortable, and at peace becomes essential. These sanctuaries are not just shelters from external stressors but are foundational to fostering your recovery and growth. They offer you the privacy to reflect, the tranquility to heal, and the freedom to grow.

Importance of Safe Spaces

In the aftermath of any traumatic experience, the need for safety—both physical and emotional—is paramount. Safe spaces provide a retreat where you can feel free to expose your vulnerabilities without fear of judgment or harm. These environments allow you to decompress, process emotions at your own pace, and start piecing together your sense of self that might have been eroded. Especially critical is the feeling of control over your environment, which often gets compromised in toxic relationships where your partner may routinely cross boundaries. Establishing a space where you dictate the terms and feel unconditionally accepted can significantly empower you to recover.

Community Resources

Community resources can be invaluable in providing safe spaces that extend beyond your immediate environment. Many communities offer centers or programs specifically designed for individuals recovering from abusive or toxic relationships. These can range from local shelters offering temporary housing to community centers providing therapy sessions, support groups, and wellness activities like yoga or meditation classes. Libraries also often serve as quiet, safe spaces to read or participate in community-led events. Engaging with these resources provides physical spaces for healing. It helps you feel supported by a network of individuals who understand and affirm what you are going through.

Creating a Safe Home Environment

Transforming your home into a healing sanctuary involves more than physical security; it requires creating an environment supporting your emotional well-being. Start by personalizing your space with things that bring you comfort and joy—photos of happy memories, artwork that inspires you, or even a playlist of soothing music. Consider the layout and aesthetics of your home; organized and clutter-free spaces can significantly reduce anxiety and promote a sense of calm. Introduce elements of nature—like plants or flowers—as they help reduce stress and boost mood. Lighting also plays a critical role in influencing your environment's feel; soft, warm lighting can make your space feel cozy and inviting. Remember, this is your retreat; each choice should contribute to a nurturing atmosphere where you can truly relax and find peace.

Online and Digital Safe Spaces

Digital platforms can also serve as vital safe spaces in today's connected world. Online support groups, forums, and social media pages dedicated to healing from toxic relationships can offer solace and solidarity. These platforms allow you to connect with others who have similar experiences, share stories, and exchange coping strategies, all from the safety and privacy of your home. However, navigating these spaces cautiously and prioritizing well-moderated platforms that make you feel supported and uplifted is essential. If specific discussions trigger negative emotions, allow yourself to step back and disengage. Your digital well-being is just as important as your physical and emotional health.

Creating and maintaining these safe spaces is a dynamic and ongoing process. As you evolve and your needs change, so too might the qualities that make a space feel safe. Continually assessing and adjusting your environments to suit your journey ensures that your healing spaces grow with you, providing comfort and support at every step.

As this chapter concludes, remember that the safe spaces you curate—physical, community-based, or digital—are not just places of refuge. They are active participants in your healing process, settings where you can reclaim your peace and power. Each environment holds the potential to reflect and reinforce your journey of recovery and self-discovery, supporting you as you rebuild a life marked by safety, respect, and fulfillment. As we transition to the next chapter, we carry forward the understanding that our environments significantly influence our healing trajectories, and we continue to explore how reconnecting with the world around us can foster further growth and healing.

7

The Healing Journey

Amid the aftermath of separation from a toxic relationship, the path to healing may seem strewn with obstacles. Yet, it is ripe with profound opportunities for growth and rejuvenation. Imagine standing at the shoreline of your existence, watching the tides of past pains recede, gradually revealing the pristine sands of your soul that await your rediscovery and care. This chapter is dedicated to guiding you through the enriching practice of self-care, an essential component of your healing journey, nurturing your mind, body, and soul in harmonious synchrony.

The Art of Self-Care: Healing Practices for Mind, Body, and Soul

Holistic Healing

True healing is holistic—it encompasses your entire being, addressing the needs of your mind, body, and soul. Each component is interconnected; neglecting one can impact the others, much like a symphony missing a section of instruments. Holistic healing begins with recognizing that your well-being depends on the balance and health of all parts of yourself. It's about creating a symphony of wellness where each part of you plays its tune harmoniously. This approach not only helps in recovering from the immediate impacts of toxic relationships but also builds resilience against future emotional disruptions.

Self-Care Techniques

Often, one thinks of self-care as indulging in a hot bath or treating yourself to a spa day—and while these can be part of caring for yourself, effective self-care encompasses a broader range of practices that nurture your entire being. Let's explore several techniques:

- **Mindfulness and Meditation:** These practices anchor you in the present moment, helping to dissipate the anxiety and stress that linger from past traumas. By focusing on your breath or quietly meditating on your thoughts and feelings without judgment, you create a space of calmness and clarity within your mind.
- **Physical Exercise:** Regular physical activity is pivotal. It could be yoga, which harmonizes body and mind, or more vigorous exercises like jogging or cycling, which enhance physical stamina and trigger endorphin release, uplifting your mood.
- **Healthy Eating:** Nourishing your body with balanced, wholesome meals can profoundly affect your emotional state. Foods rich in omega-3 fatty acids, for instance, are known to boost brain function and enhance mood.

Creating a Self-Care Routine

Crafting a self-care routine that resonates with your lifestyle is like planting a garden tailored to your aesthetic and environmental conditions. It requires thoughtful consideration of what practices nourish you and fit into your daily life. Start small: Integrate a ten-minute meditation into your morning routine, or swap out one processed meal daily for something organic and whole. As these small changes become habitual, they lay down the patterns for more extensive, sustainable practices that keep you grounded and focused on healing.

The Role of Nature and Art in Healing

Engaging with nature and art offers therapeutic experiences that can significantly aid your healing process. Nature, with its inherent beauty and rhythm, has a way of imparting peace and perspective. Activities like hiking through a forest, walking along a beach, or simply sitting in a park and observing the natural flow of life can be incredibly restorative. Similarly, art provides a conduit for expressing complex emotions and untangling deep-seated thoughts. Whether painting, writing, sculpting, or engaging in any creative endeavor, art allows you to externalize feelings that may be too difficult to articulate, facilitating a profound form of emotional release.

Reflective Journaling Prompt: Design Your Ideal Day of Self-Care

To deepen your engagement with self-care, take a moment to journal about your ideal day of self-care. What activities would you include? How would these activities nourish different aspects of your being? This exercise helps you visualize a comprehensive approach to self-care and serves as a blueprint for integrating these practices into your routine. Consider this journaling prompt a personal workshop where you can creatively plan the restoration of your well-being.

As you embrace these self-care strategies, remember that each small step is part of a more significant journey toward a renewed, empowered self. By nurturing your mind, body, and soul with kindness and understanding, you rebuild the inner strength necessary to thrive beyond the shadows of past relationships.

Rediscovering Self: Identity After Toxicity

In the aftermath of a toxic relationship, you may often find that not only has the relationship been draining, but it also, quite insidiously, eroded pieces of your essential self. The person you once knew—your dreams, desires, and personal quirks—might seem obscured or altered. Rediscovering and reclaiming your sense of self is not just about recovery; it's about giving yourself permission to meet, know, and love yourself all over again. This reacquaintance is a gentle process of exploration, a way to welcome back the parts of your persona overshadowed by another's needs and manipulations.

The journey to self-reclamation often begins with the simple yet profound act of journaling. This age-old practice offers a private, unfiltered medium to dialogue with your innermost thoughts and feelings. Start by writing about your experiences in the toxic relationship, acknowledging the pain and the change it wrought in you. Then, gently shift your focus to who you are outside that context. What are your foundational likes and dislikes? What activities light up your spirit? What values do you hold dear? Journaling these reflections can gradually peel away the layers of confusion left by toxicity, revealing the core of your true self.

Exploring new hobbies or revisiting old ones can also be incredibly illuminating. Perhaps you once loved to paint, play an instrument, or garden—activities that you may have pushed aside. Reengage with these passions or discover new ones. Learning and engaging in something purely for your enjoyment is a powerful affirmation of your individuality. It reinforces your right to personal space and pleasure. These are areas that you often compromise in toxic dynamics. Moreover, hobbies can serve as a therapeutic outlet, offering a way to express and process complex emotions in a constructive and rewarding manner.

Solo travel represents another avenue for self-discovery that pushes the boundaries of your comfort zone and accelerates personal growth. Traveling alone challenges you to navigate new environments, make decisions independently, and meet new people, which can boost your confidence and self-reliance. Each decision made, and each interaction navigated reaffirm your capability and independence. Choose destinations that resonate with your interests or offer experiences you've always wanted to explore. Whether it's a quiet retreat into nature, a cultural immersion in a bustling city, or a spiritual journey in a sacred space, travel can profoundly shift your perspective, helping you to see yourself and the world in a new light.

Celebrating your individuality is an essential step in solidifying your reclaimed identity. Do not just recognize but also delight in the qualities and strengths that make you unique. Embrace your quirks, those aspects of your character that were misunderstood or undervalued in your past relationship. It could be your unconventional sense of humor, intense passion for niche subjects, or creative way of solving problems. Whatever these traits may be, recognize them as assets, not liabilities. Celebrate them with others who appreciate and encourage your authentic self. This celebration is not just about accepting who you are; it's about reveling in your uniqueness and recognizing that the very traits that make you different are the ones that make you extraordinary.

Building a new self-concept after a toxic relationship involves both introspection and outward expression. It's about piecing together the fragmented parts of your identity and presenting them to the world with confidence. Surround yourself with people who support and uplift you and encourage you to express yourself fully and without fear. Such supportive relationships reinforce your positive self-concept and help cement your identity as someone worthy of respect and love. Engage in activities that align with your values and allow you to express your true self through artistic endeavors, community service, or public speaking. Each act of expression solidifies your sense of self, helping you to stand firm in your identity, free from the shadows of past toxic relationships.

The Therapeutic Path: Choosing the Right Professional Help

When embarking on your post-toxic relationship healing path, engaging with professional therapy can be as pivotal as finding a safe harbor during a storm. Therapy offers a structured environment where you can unpack the emotional baggage carried from toxic relationships under the guidance of someone trained to navigate such turbulent waters. Various types of therapy and counseling can serve different aspects of your healing, depending on your personal experiences and the nature of the traumas endured.

Cognitive Behavioral Therapy (CBT) is particularly beneficial for individuals coming out of manipulative relationships as it focuses on changing specific negative thought patterns. Through CBT, you can learn to identify and challenge the destructive beliefs that a toxic relationship may have instilled in you, such as feelings of worthlessness or powerlessness, and replace them with healthier, more constructive thoughts. Another potent form of therapy is Dialectical Behavior Therapy (DBT), which is effective in teaching skills to manage painful emotions and decrease conflict in relationships. DBT emphasizes balancing acceptance and change, helping you accept your past experiences while working to change your emotional reactions and relationship behaviors moving forward.

Psychodynamic therapy delves into the deeper, often subconscious, roots of emotional suffering. It can be particularly insightful for those who find themselves repeatedly drawn into toxic relationships, as it seeks to uncover early childhood influences and unresolved conflicts that may be shaping your current relationship choices. This form of therapy can provide profound insights into your emotional world, helping to understand and heal the foundational wounds that predispose you to toxic dynamics.

Finding the right therapist is as crucial as choosing the type of therapy. Feeling a sense of trust and safety with your therapist is essential, as the therapeutic relationship itself can significantly impact your healing process. Start by researching therapists who specialize in dealing with trauma and toxic relationship recovery. Many therapists offer an initial consultation, an excellent opportunity to gauge how comfortable you feel with them. During this meeting, ask about their experience with situations like yours, their approach to therapy, and what type of outcomes you might expect. They must listen to you without judgment and demonstrate understanding and empathy towards your experiences.

Alternative Therapies: Broadening the Healing Spectrum

In addition to traditional talk therapies, alternative therapies offer complementary ways of healing that can engage different parts of your mind and body. Art therapy, for instance, allows you to express emotions that might be too difficult to articulate in words. Through creating art, you can explore complex feelings like anger, sadness, or betrayal in a tangible form, which can be incredibly cathartic and enlightening. This therapy benefits those who naturally gravitate towards visual or firsthand expressions.

Animal-assisted therapy is another enriching alternative that involves interaction with animals, such as dogs, horses, or even dolphins, to help improve your mental health. Animals are known for their unconditional acceptance and present-moment awareness, which can be remarkably soothing for individuals, healing from emotional abuse or neglect. Engaging with animals can help rebuild trust and alleviate loneliness or isolation.

Mindfulness-based stress reduction (MBSR) programs teach mindfulness techniques to help you become more aware of the present moment and less caught up in negative thought loops. This therapy is grounded in mindfulness meditation, yoga, and body awareness exercises. MBSR can be particularly effective in managing anxiety and depressive symptoms that often accompany the aftermath of toxic relationships, helping you cultivate a state of calm and centeredness amidst life's stresses.

The Importance of Commitment: Embracing the Therapeutic Journey

Commitment to the therapeutic process is essential for proper healing to occur. Therapy is not a quick fix but a gradual journey towards deeper self-awareness and change. It requires openness to exploring painful truths and willingness to modify deeply ingrained patterns of thinking and behaving. Being fully committed means attending sessions regularly, actively engaging in the discussions, and doing any homework or practice exercises your therapist suggests. Remember, your work outside the therapy sessions is just as important as your work during them.

As you continue on this path, consider each therapy session a steppingstone toward a more insightful and empowered self. With each step, you move away from the shadows of your past and toward a lighter, more liberated existence where you can live out your true potential and form healthier, more fulfilling relationships.

Cultivating Healthy Relationships: Learning from the Past

Reflecting on past relationships, especially those that have drained or hurt us, often feels like reopening old wounds. Yet, this reflection is not about dwelling on the pain but mining these experiences for valuable insights that can lead to healthier, more fulfilling relationships in the future. Each relationship, regardless of its outcome, comes with lessons about what you value, what you can tolerate, and what you fundamentally need from your interactions with others.

When you dissect the dynamics of past toxic relationships, you begin to see patterns—perhaps a tendency to prioritize the other's needs over your own or ignore red flags because of a deep-seated fear of loneliness. Recognizing these patterns is the first step in breaking them. It involves an honest assessment of your role in these dynamics, not to assign blame to yourself but to empower you with the knowledge to make different choices moving forward. For instance, if you often silence your voice to avoid conflict, acknowledging this can be the impetus for practicing assertiveness. You might begin with small, low-stakes situations, gradually building up your confidence to express your thoughts and needs more openly in more significant relationships.

As you move towards forming new relationships, understanding, and embodying the qualities of healthy relationships is necessary. Healthy relationships are typically marked by mutual respect, trust, and open communication. Mutual respect involves recognizing and valuing each other's differences and treating one another with kindness and consideration without conditions. Trust, on the other hand, must be built over time—it's the belief that you can rely on the other person to act with your best interests at heart, just as they believe the same of you. This trust grows from consistent actions that match words, creating a stable foundation for the relationship. Open communication is perhaps the most vital element; it's the conduit through which your needs, thoughts, and feelings are shared. Healthy communication involves transparent, honest, and respectful exchanges where both parties feel heard and validated.

Building trust in new relationships while maintaining healthy boundaries can often feel like walking a tightrope. On one side, there's the vulnerability that comes with opening up to someone new, and on the other, the need to protect oneself from potential hurt. One strategy for navigating this is to adopt a gradual approach to sharing personal information and intimacy. Share small, less consequential things initially and observe how the other person responds. Do they respect your privacy? Do they reciprocate by sharing things about themselves as well? As a deeper relationship develops, their reactions can provide clues about their trustworthiness and suitability.

The role of emotional intelligence in fostering healthy relationships is pivotal. Emotional intelligence involves being aware of and in control of your emotions and understanding the feelings of others. In relationships, this skill allows you to navigate interactions with empathy and clarity. For example, suppose a partner is going through a tough time. In that case, emotional intelligence will enable you to perceive their mood and needs without them having to spell it out explicitly. Conversely, it also means recognizing and communicating your emotional states during difficult times, preventing misunderstandings, and fostering mutual support. Cultivating emotional intelligence involves regular self-reflection, seeking feedback from trusted friends or mentors, and, if needed, collaborating with a therapist who can help you understand and manage your emotions more effectively.

As you apply these insights and strategies, you gradually learn to form relationships that are not only supportive and enriching but also reflective of the love and respect you deserve. These relationships, built on mutual respect, trust, and healthy communication, allow you to thrive and bring your best self to your romantic partnerships and all your interpersonal connections.

Setting New Boundaries: Lessons Learned

In the wake of a toxic relationship, one of the most empowering steps you can take is learning how to establish and maintain healthy boundaries. Think of boundaries as personal property lines that define where your emotional and physical space begins and ends. They help you navigate interactions by clearly stating what is acceptable and what is not, ensuring that your relationships—platonic, familial, or romantic—develop respectfully and healthily. Learning from past toxic relationships, where these boundaries were likely blurred or disregarded, provides a crucial foundation for understanding your needs and limits moving forward.

Setting new boundaries is an act of self-respect and an assertion of your rights. It involves introspection and sometimes challenging work, as you need to identify what you value and desire and what you can no longer tolerate. You can go from not accepting disrespectful language to deciding how much personal information you share with others. You should understand that while you created these boundaries because of past relationships, they are not about building walls. Instead, they're about building bridges to healthier interactions. For example, suppose constant texting was a tool of control in your past relationship. In that case, you might set a new boundary around digital communication, specifying times or frequencies that are comfortable for you.

To have your boundaries respected by others, they must be crystal clear. Clarity and assertiveness are your allies when introducing new boundaries to acquaintances, friends, or romantic partners. Start by expressing your needs calmly and clearly. For instance, if you decide you need some time to yourself after work to decompress, you might say, "I value our time together, but I need about an hour to myself after work to relax. I would appreciate it if we could plan our conversations or meetings after that time." This statement is direct and respectful, giving the other person a clear understanding of your needs without being confrontational. It's also important to be consistent in enforcing these boundaries. Consistency sends a message that you are serious about your needs, which helps others to respect them more readily.

Respecting your boundaries is just as crucial as setting them. Often, we can be our worst enemies by setting limits and then allowing ourselves to overstep them to please others or avoid conflict. This self-compromise can be damaging, as it sends a mixed signal to yourself and others about your values and limits. To stay true to your boundaries, remind yourself why they are essential. Reflect on the consequences of not respecting these boundaries in the past and their impact on your mental and emotional well-being. Keeping these reflections in mind can help you maintain the commitment to honor your boundaries, even when it might be uncomfortable.

Dealing with challenges and pushbacks is an inevitable part of setting new boundaries, especially for those who may have benefited from your previous lack of limits. When faced with resistance, reinforce your boundaries with calm and firm responses. Suppose someone continues to challenge a boundary despite clear communication. In that case, it may be necessary to evaluate the role they play in your life. Are they respecting your right to personal space and well-being? Maintaining healthy boundaries might sometimes mean reducing contact with those who consistently disregard them or, in extreme cases, ending relationships. While this can be difficult, protecting your emotional health and upholding the standards you've set for your interactions is sometimes necessary.

As you navigate this process of setting and maintaining new boundaries, remember that each interaction is an opportunity to affirm your self-worth and foster healthier, more respectful relationships. These boundaries aren't just protective measures; they affirm your growth and commitment to never settle for less than you deserve.

Embracing Solitude: The Power of Being Single

In the quiet after the storm of a toxic relationship, solitude often wraps around you like a soft, albeit unfamiliar, blanket. While initially daunting, this solitude holds profound opportunities for personal growth, independence, and a deep-seated peace that comes from reconnecting with your inner self. Often, society paints solitude as a state to be remedied—filled with friends, lovers, noise, and haste. Yet, when embraced, solitude becomes a sanctuary where the deepest voices of your heart are heard most clearly.

One of the most transformative benefits of embracing solitude is the journey of self-discovery it initiates. Free from the influence and demands of a partner, you have the unique opportunity to explore your desires, fears, aspirations, and dreams without compromise or distraction. This exploration is not about loneliness but about fostering a fulfilling relationship with yourself. Imagine having the space to listen to your thoughts without interruption and learn what makes you feel alive, fulfilled, or serene. This period of solitude can help you redefine your goals and values based on your individual preferences, not shaped by the dynamics of a past relationship that may have clouded your true self.

Solo activities can play a vital role in this self-discovery. Consider, for example, the simple act of traveling alone, whether it's a day trip to a nearby town or a longer journey to a foreign land; traveling solo forces you out of your comfort zone and challenges you to engage with the world directly. Every decision—from where to eat to what sights to see—is yours, reinforcing your independence and decision-making skills. Similarly, attending workshops or classes that pique your interest, be it photography, cooking, or writing, can enrich your life in unexpected ways. These activities introduce you to new skills and hobbies and connect you with like-minded individuals who share your passions, expanding your social circle in meaningful ways.

The challenge, however, lies in overcoming the fear and societal stigma associated with being single. Too often, solitude is equated with loneliness, a notion fueled by cultural narratives prioritizing romantic relationships as the pinnacle of personal happiness. To counter this, it's better to cultivate a mindset that views solitude as an opportunity for growth and self-care. Start by affirming the positives of solitude—peace, freedom, and the space to grow. Reflect on how these aspects contribute to your well-being and write them down as reminders for moments when solitude feels more like isolation than liberation.

Celebrating singlehood is an act of defiance against societal expectations and a celebration of self-sufficiency. It's about taking pride in your ability to enjoy your own company and manage your life independently. Organize days that are entirely about self-indulgence—perhaps starting with a morning walk, followed by a visit to your favorite café, and ending with an evening at a concert or treating yourself to a movie. When savored alone, these moments reinforce the joy and contentment that can come from being your best company.

As this chapter of embracing solitude concludes, reflect on the profound peace of being comfortable in your presence. Consider solitude not as a gap between relationships but a fulfilling phase of life where personal growth and independence take center stage. This time is not about waiting for something or someone but about enriching the person you are, cultivating a life that feels rewarding and complete on its terms. As you continue to explore and enjoy this phase, remember that the relationship you build with yourself is the foundation upon which all other relationships are built. Embrace this time enthusiastically and see it as integral to your journey towards a happier, more fulfilled you.

8

Thriving After Toxicity

I magine yourself as a tree exposed to harsh weather, its leaves battered yet still standing resiliently; this resilience isn't just about survival but about thriving—growing new leaves, reaching higher towards the sunlight. As you step away from the shadows cast by toxic relationships, you carry the strength forged through adversity, ready to blossom anew. This chapter is dedicated to nurturing that strength, transforming the resilience developed in the storm into a vibrant canopy that shelters and enriches your life.

Building Emotional Resilience: Strategies for Strength

Defining Emotional Resilience

Emotional resilience refers to the ability to bounce back from stress, adversity, failure, challenges, or trauma. It's not about avoiding the distress or denying its effects but instead facing them head-on, equipped with strategies that allow you to learn, grow, and emerge stronger from the experiences. In recovering from toxic relationships, resilience becomes a cornerstone for rebuilding your life. The inner strength supports you in confronting painful memories and ongoing challenges, encouraging a mindset that views obstacles as opportunities for growth.

Practices for Building Resilience

Building resilience is akin to muscle strengthening; it requires consistent effort and the proper techniques. One powerful method is cognitive reframing, which involves changing your perspective on adverse events and viewing them as opportunities rather than obstacles. For instance, instead of seeing the end of a toxic relationship as a failure, you can reframe it as a courageous step towards self-respect and a new beginning.

Stress management techniques also play a crucial role in cultivating resilience. Practices such as deep breathing exercises, progressive muscle relaxation, or mindfulness meditation can help reduce stress's physiological and psychological impacts. Integrating these practices into your daily routine creates a buffer against the stressors that life throws your way, enabling you to respond with calmness and clarity.

Cultivating optimism is another key element in building resilience. Don't think it means you should ignore reality; instead, you should focus on your life's positive aspects. Start by acknowledging small victories and positive moments each day. It could be as simple as enjoying a peaceful cup of coffee, a call from a friend, or a job well done. Focusing on these positives reinforces a sense of accomplishment and satisfaction that can buoy you through more challenging times.

The Role of Support Networks

No tree stands alone in a forest; building resilience is not a solitary journey. A robust support network is vital, providing emotional comfort, practical help, and a different perspective on challenges. To enhance your resilience, actively seek out and engage with supportive communities. These include therapy groups, online forums dedicated to personal growth, or local clubs and organizations that align with your interests.

Engaging with these communities offers multiple benefits. They provide a sense of belonging, reduce feelings of isolation, and offer diverse viewpoints and coping strategies that can enrich one's approach to challenges. Moreover, as one contributes one's experiences and support to the group, one reinforces one's sense of purpose and self-worth, key components of resilience.

Resilience and Future Challenges

As you build your resilience, you equip yourself to face future challenges with a fortified spirit. This resilience ensures that when faced with stress or adversity, you have a wellspring of strength to tap into, allowing you to oversee crises more effectively and emerge with fewer scars. It's about moving forward confidently, knowing you have the tools and the fortitude to navigate whatever paths lie ahead.

Building resilience is ultimately about cultivating a deep-seated strength that supports your overall well-being and propels you toward a thriving life. It's a dynamic process that you can continually develop and refine as you encounter new experiences and challenges. By investing in your resilience, you are not just preparing to survive future storms—you are preparing to grow lush and full, grounded in the knowledge that you have the strength to withstand the winds and flourish.

Finding Joy and Purpose: Life Beyond Toxicity

Rediscovering joy after the end of a toxic relationship can feel like waking up to the first rays of the sun after a long night. It's about allowing yourself to feel and relish life's simple pleasures once more truly. Often, in the throes of challenging times, you might have muted these vibrant parts of your existence to cope with the ongoing stress. As you move beyond those shadows, it's time to rekindle the joy in everyday moments and activities. Start small— notice the warmth of a sunbeam on your skin, the taste of your favorite food, or the comfort of a soft blanket. These small acknowledgments are like whispers of life's pleasures, calling you back to a fuller appreciation of the world.

Reviving old hobbies or discovering new interests plays a crucial role in this rejuvenation. Think back to activities that once sparked a light in you, perhaps before or during the early stages of the toxicity that later clouded your relationship. Did you enjoy painting? Were you an avid reader, a hiker, or perhaps a musician? Revisit these passions without the pressure to perform or excel— simply for the joy they bring. If your old hobbies don't ignite the same happiness or if they get back painful memories, venture into new territories. Learning something new, be it cooking a different cuisine, starting a blog, or practicing yoga, can be a source of joy and a powerful affirmation of your growth and independence.

Pursuing passions and defining your purpose extends beyond hobbies and encompasses your broader existential and professional contributions. Reflect on what you feel enthusiastic about—issues that stir your heart and stir your mind to action. Your interest could include anything from animal welfare and education to environmental activism. Engaging in activities that align with these passions can imbue your life with a profound sense of purpose and fulfillment. Moreover, integrating your passions into your professional life can transform your work from a mere job to a calling. Consider how your strengths and interests can address the needs you see in the world. You might need to shift careers, go back to school, or start a new business that aligns more closely with your areas of passion.

Setting and achieving goals is another vital aspect of rediscovering joy and purpose. Goals give you a sense of direction and an endpoint to strive towards, which can be incredibly motivating and rewarding. Start by setting clear, achievable goals, both short-term and long-term. Use the SMART criteria—Specific, Measurable, Achievable, Relevant, Time-bound—to guide your goal-setting process. For example, if you wish to integrate more creativity into your life, a specific goal could be to complete a painting over the next three weeks. Keep track of your progress, and celebrate your achievements, no matter how small. These activities will boost your morale and make you feel more capable, reminding you of your growth and progress.

Practicing gratitude is integral to rediscovering joy. It shifts your focus from what's missing or has been difficult in your life to the abundance that exists and often goes unnoticed. Begin or end each day by listing three things you're grateful for. These could be as simple as a delicious meal, a call from a friend, or even the progress you've made in your healing process. Over time, this practice can significantly alter your perception, helping you see the world and your life as a glass half full rather than half empty. It cultivates a habit of seeking out and appreciating the good, which can be incredibly uplifting and transformative, especially after prolonged negativity.

As you engage in these activities—pursuing passions, setting goals, and practicing gratitude—you weave a richer, more colorful tapestry of life. Each thread represents a choice, moment, or relationship you've consciously chosen to bring into your life, crafting a future that resonates with who you are and aspires to be.

This tapestry, continuously expanding and evolving, symbolizes a life lived not just in the absence of toxicity but in the presence of deliberate and cultivated joy.

Navigating New Relationships: Red Flags and Green Flags

Embarking on new relationships after experiencing toxic ones can feel like cautiously stepping back into the water after a storm has passed. Feeling excitement and apprehension is natural; these feelings are valid and reflect a desire to move forward mindfully, ensuring your future relationships are healthy and supportive. As you navigate these new waters, it's crucial to understand the signs —warning signals (red flags) and positive indicators (green flags) that can guide your decisions about whom to let into your life.

Recognizing Red Flags

Red flags in a relationship often manifest subtly before becoming more apparent. They are early warning signs that the person may not be conducive to a healthy relationship. One typical red flag is a disregard for your boundaries. Suppose someone consistently pushes against or ignores your set limits, whether emotionally, physically, or digitally. In that case, it signals a lack of respect for your personal space and autonomy. Another significant red flag is the presence of controlling behaviors. This can range from dictating who you should spend time with to making decisions about your personal or financial matters without your consent. Excessive jealousy or possessiveness can also be early indicators of potentially manipulative and controlling behavior. These signs are particularly crucial to heed if you've experienced similar patterns in past toxic relationships.

It's also important to watch for how someone manages disagreements or conflicts. Communication during these times can be very telling. Consider this a major red flag if the person resorts to belittling, gaslighting, or aggressive behaviors instead of constructive discussion. Such behaviors suggest an inability to manage conflict healthily, essential for a supportive, long-term relationship. Pay attention to your emotions after interactions; feeling drained, anxious, or unhappy consistently can indicate that the relationship negatively impacts your emotional well-being.

Understanding Green Flags

Just as crucial as recognizing red flags, identifying green flags can reassure you that a relationship is moving in a healthy direction. One of the most significant green flags is consistent respect for your boundaries. A partner who listens to and honors your limits without pushing them demonstrates a healthy respect for your individuality. Another positive indicator is open and honest communication. A partner who expresses their feelings and thoughts openly and respects your input creates a foundation for mutual trust and understanding.

Additionally, look for signs of emotional maturity, such as taking responsibility for actions, apologizing when wrong, and handling disagreements calmly and respectfully. These behaviors indicate a person's ability to contribute positively to a relationship's health and longevity. Also, a partner who encourages your personal growth and supports your interests without feeling threatened or jealous is showing a green flag. This support can manifest in celebrating your successes, encouraging you to pursue your goals, and comforting you without trying to fix every issue.

Pacing New Relationships

After leaving a toxic relationship, you might have an urge to fill the void or find validation quickly. However, rushing into a new relationship without fully understanding the person can lead you back into unhealthy patterns. Take the time to get to know someone honestly. It involves observing their behavior in various situations over time and in different contexts, such as with friends and family and during stress. Pacing the relationship allows you to build trust gradually and see if their actions consistently match their words, which is crucial for establishing a healthy, long-term relationship.

Trust and Intuition

Your intuition is a powerful ally in navigating new relationships. Our gut feelings can often pick up on red flags before we consciously acknowledge them. Trusting your intuition means listening to those subtle internal cues that alert you when something doesn't feel right. This does not mean jumping to conclusions without evidence but instead paying attention to your instincts and considering them seriously, especially if they persist. Your past experiences have likely honed your ability to detect warning signs early on. Trust that these instincts protect and guide you towards healthier relationship choices.

As you move forward, remember that building new relationships is a process of learning and growth. Each interaction teaches you more about others and yourself, helping you form deeper, more meaningful connections that enrich your life and foster a sense of mutual respect and understanding. These relationships, built on a foundation of respect, communication, and genuine support, will thrive, bringing joy and companionship into your life in a way that honors your journey and the person you have become.

The Role of Forgiveness in Healing: To Forgive or Not?

Forgiveness is a theme often woven into discussions about healing, especially when it comes to moving past the pain of toxic relationships. It's essential to explore what forgiveness entails and how it can function as a tool—not just for closing chapters but for healing them. In this context, forgiveness isn't about condoning hurtful behaviors or diminishing your experiences. Instead, it is about freeing yourself from the heavy chains of bitterness and resentment that can tether you to the past, draining your emotional energy and potentially hindering your recovery.

At its core, forgiveness is about personal peace. It involves reaching a state where the actions of another no longer control your emotional well-being. You may not forget the past, or the memories may not cease to sting, but instead, they lose their power to disrupt your peace. It's a profound shift from heartache to a focus on personal growth and happiness. However, embracing forgiveness can be challenging. It often requires ample time and reflection, and most importantly, it should be a choice that comes from deep within you, not imposed by external expectations or societal pressures. This choice is nuanced and deeply personal, often accompanied by relief and apprehension as you step into a space of vulnerability.

An essential distinction to understand in the healing process is forgiveness and reconciliation. Forgiving someone does not automatically entail re-establishing a relationship with them. You can forgive someone and choose not to have them in your life. Reconciliation might require ongoing interaction and a rebuilding of trust, which is not always possible or healthy, particularly in cases of toxic relationships. Forgiveness is for you—it is about setting your heart free from anger, while reconciliation is about jointly mending a relationship and is not always advisable or necessary.

Self-forgiveness is another crucial aspect of healing, often overlooked in the recovery process. Reflecting on your experiences in a toxic relationship might lead you to harbor guilt or blame for the things that happened or for staying too long. Extending compassion to yourself is vital, as well as understanding that manipulation and coercion can cloud judgment and make it extremely difficult to leave such relationships. Forgiving yourself is acknowledging that you did the best you could with the knowledge and resources available to you. It's about recognizing that your past does not define your worth or your future.

Viewing forgiveness as a personal journey underscores its role as a process rather than a one-time act. It's a path you choose when you feel ready, and it evolves with you. Some days, forgiveness might feel within easy reach; on others, forgiveness might seem miles away. This ebb and flow is usual as you commit to moving forward at your own pace, without pressure. This journey is about letting go of the pain caused by others and reclaiming your inner peace and power. It's about learning to live with the memories without letting them control your emotional landscape.

As you consider integrating forgiveness into your healing process, remember it's okay to protect your peace first. If forgiveness feels too challenging now, allow yourself the space to heal in other ways —through therapy, through self-care, and through new experiences that affirm your worth. Forgiveness may or may not be a part of your healing journey, and neither is perfectly acceptable. Your healing is about you and your need to move forward on your terms with grace and strength.

Creating a Legacy of Empowerment: Sharing Your Story

Sharing your story, especially one that involves overcoming the darkness of a toxic relationship, is much more than recounting past events. It is an act of empowerment, a profound declaration that you have survived and gained invaluable insights and strength from your experiences. When you share your journey, you do more than speak your truth—you transform your narrative into a vessel of hope and guidance for others. This process can significantly amplify your healing, reinforcing your self-worth and accomplishment. As you articulate the challenges you faced and the steps you took to overcome them, you reinforce the reality of your achievements. It's a reaffirmation of your resilience and strength, which can inspire a renewed sense of purpose and empowerment in your life.

Numerous platforms are available for sharing your story, each offering unique opportunities to reach and connect with others. Whether through blog posts, articles, or even a book, writing allows for deep reflection and a permanent record of your journey that can reach a broad audience. Personal blogs and websites will enable you to control your narrative and engage directly with your audience. For those who prefer speaking, public speaking engagements, podcasts, or interviews offer a platform to share your story verbally. These platforms allow you to reach others and refine your understanding of your own experiences through the questions and interactions they prompt.

Social media platforms like Instagram, Facebook, and Twitter also offer influential venues for storytelling. Here, you can share snippets of your journey, interact with a community, and join broader conversations about recovery from toxic relationships. Additionally, support groups, whether online or in person, provide a more intimate setting for sharing. These groups offer a safe space where members can relate deeply to their experiences, providing mutual support and understanding. In these settings, your story can give tangible hope and practical advice to those still in the thick of their struggles.

While sharing your story can be incredibly empowering, navigating this process with careful consideration for your privacy and emotional safety is essential. Setting boundaries around what you choose to share is crucial. Decide in advance which aspects of your story you are comfortable sharing and which parts you prefer to keep private. It's okay to say that specific topics or questions are off-limits. Speaking your mind protects your emotional health and empowers you to control the narrative. It's also wise to consider the potential impact of revisiting traumatic events on your well-being. If sharing specific details makes you feel vulnerable or distressed, it might be beneficial to withhold those elements, focus on the lessons learned, or discuss your healing process instead.

When choosing the platform for sharing your story, consider the audience and the level of interaction you are comfortable with. For example, a blog or a public speaking engagement might reach a wider audience with less personal interaction. In contrast, support groups offer more direct feedback and engagement. Each platform has its potential benefits and risks, and what works for one person may not be ideal for another. It's about finding a balance that feels right for you, where sharing feels safe and constructive.

Sharing your story is not just about recounting the past; it's about crafting a narrative of empowerment. It's an opportunity to own your experiences, speak about them on your terms, and highlight the strengths you've gained. This process can undoubtedly inspire others, but more importantly, it can reaffirm your growth and resilience. By choosing how, where, and when to share your journey, you assert control over your life's narrative, turning your past experiences into a beacon of hope for others and a testament to your strength and recovery.

The Ongoing Journey: Maintaining Your Progress and Embracing Future Challenges

Life after a toxic relationship isn't a finite process with a clear endpoint; instead, it unfolds continuously, a path of ongoing growth, learning, and self-discovery. Your path is paved with daily choices contributing to your well-being and challenges, testing your resilience and growth. Think of it as tending to a garden; it requires regular nurturing, occasional pruning, and constant care to thrive.

Regular self-reflection is one of the most vital practices in maintaining your emotional health. Self-reflection involves consciously considering your thoughts, feelings, and behaviors. Self-reflection helps you understand your emotional triggers and the progress you've made, and it allows you to align your actions with your values and goals. This could be as structured as scheduled journaling sessions where you delve into your reactions to recent events or as spontaneous as meditative moments where you mentally review your day before sleeping. The key is consistency—making self-reflection a regular part of your routine ensures that you remain actively engaged with your emotional health and are prepared to address issues as they arise.

Continuing therapy can play a crucial role in this ongoing process. A therapist acts as a guide through difficult times and as a sounding board for your thoughts and feelings. As you encounter new challenges or milestones, your therapist can provide the perspective and tools needed to navigate them. This might involve adjusting coping strategies as your life changes or exploring deeper psychological patterns that emerge over time. You should view therapy as a remedy for difficult times and as a consistent part of your emotional wellness practice.

Self-care also remains a cornerstone of maintaining emotional health. By now, you've likely identified practices supporting your well—being— yoga, reading, hiking, or spending time with loved ones. Continuing to prioritize these activities is crucial. They serve not only as enjoyable experiences but also as essential components of your mental and emotional stability. They are your reservoirs of peace and joy, resources you can draw on during more challenging times. Moreover, integrating new self-care practices as you grow, and your needs change keeps your approach to well-being dynamic and responsive to your evolving life.

Facing future challenges with resilience and the lessons learned from past experiences equips you to manage life's uncertainties more grounded and confidently. Each challenge, whether a complex work project, personal setback, or new relationship dynamic, tests your built resilience. These experiences are obstacles and opportunities to apply what you've learned about managing stress, setting boundaries, and maintaining emotional equilibrium. They are real-time applications of your growing skills and resilience, each one an opportunity to refine and strengthen your abilities.

The mindset of continued growth and learning ensures that your healing and development are lifelong processes. It's about embracing the idea that growth has yet to reach a final destination or ultimate peak. Instead, it's about continually striving to understand, live more fully, and respond more effectively to the world around you. You can actively pursue educational opportunities, seek new cultural experiences, or remain curious and open-minded in daily interactions. Each new experience and piece of knowledge contributes to a broader, richer understanding of yourself and the world, enhancing your life's texture and depth.

As this chapter in your life's book unfolds, remember that each day is a step in your journey of self-discovery and growth. The road doesn't always ascend; sometimes it plateaus, other times it dips, but each phase is integral to the larger landscape of your life. Your resilience, nurtured through self-reflection, therapy, and continual learning, prepares you to face future challenges and embrace them as catalysts for further growth, enriching your journey with each step forward.

In conclusion, this journey is not about reaching a destination but about cultivating a sustainable practice of growth, reflection, and resilience that moves you through life. As we transition into the next chapter, carry forward the understanding that each challenge and joy is a thread in the intricate tapestry of your ongoing story, each valuable and defining in its own right.

Help Others Find the Courage to Let Go

When you commit to a relationship, it's logical to do all you can to keep it alive. However, when you find that you are given more than you possibly can and that your boundaries are constantly being stepped over and disrespected, it's a sure sign that you need to take steps in a different direction. As Nina Simone once sang, "You've got to learn to leave the table when love's no longer being served."

This book has revealed that toxicity does not end the moment you walk out the door, however. Authentic healing comes from knowing yourself, so you can make better choices in the future and discover the importance of setting boundaries. If you feel this book has helped you take your first steps toward healthier relationships, please share your opinion with others.

WANT TO HELP OTHERS?

Thanks for taking the time to shine the light for someone who may think there is no way out. Let them know that freedom starts from within.

Scan the QR code below to leave a review:

Conclusion

As we reach the end of our journey together through the pages of this book, it's essential to pause and reflect on the transformative path we've traversed—from recognizing the shadows of toxicity to stepping into the empowering light of self-awareness and healing. We've explored the depths of toxic relationships, uncovered the subtle signs of manipulation and control, and armed ourselves with the knowledge to escape and heal. More importantly, we've embraced the possibility of thriving beyond the confines of past pains.

Recognizing toxic patterns early in a relationship cannot be overstated. It is the first pivotal step toward safeguarding your emotional well-being. Understanding these signs and trusting your instincts can prevent prolonged psychological harm and lead you toward healthier interpersonal dynamics. Remember, the earlier you identify these patterns, the sooner you can take steps to protect and empower yourself.

Throughout this book, I've emphasized the power of personal agency and the transformative practice of self-care. You possess the innate strength to change your circumstances. Setting boundaries and prioritizing your needs are not acts of selfishness but of self-respect. Cultivating these practices is essential for anyone looking to reclaim their peace and pave the way for a fulfilling life.

Support systems play an indispensable role in our journey of recovery and growth. Whether these are friends, family members, online communities, or support groups, the connections we forge can offer us comfort, validation, and guidance. Never underestimate the power of a supportive community to uplift and propel you forward during challenging times.

Healing and personal development are ongoing processes. Each day offers a new opportunity for growth and self-discovery. Continue to nurture your resilience and expand your horizons; let your healing journey be a continuous adventure that evolves and flourishes over time. And when the path becomes overwhelming, remember that seeking professional help is a testament to your strength and commitment to your well-being. Therapy or counseling can provide you with the tools and support needed to navigate the complexities of emotional healing.

I encourage you to share your story when you feel ready. Sharing your experiences can profoundly impact not only your healing process but also that of others who may be struggling in silence. Your voice can shine as a beacon of hope and solidarity, showing others they are not alone in their battles.

As you move forward, I challenge you to apply the lessons learned from this book to all your relationships. Strive to build connections rooted in respect, honesty, and mutual support. Whether in romance, family dynamics, friendships, or professional relationships, the principles of healthy interactions remain the same.

Trust your instincts—they are your most dependable guides through the complexities of relationships and life's decisions. Listening to and honoring your feelings can lead you toward more authentic and fulfilling experiences.

Finally, let us conclude with a message of hope and resilience. I have reiterated several concepts a few times not to be redundant but to emphasize the concepts. No matter your difficulties, there is always a path forward. A life filled with self-respect, healthy relationships, and personal fulfillment is not just a possibility but a reality within your reach. Carry forward the knowledge and insights from this book with the assurance that you have the tools to navigate whatever comes your way. Here's to a future where you survive and thrive in the radiance of your newfound strength and wisdom.

References

1. BetterUp. (n.d.). Emotional Triggers: What They Are and 9 Tips Deal With Them. Retrieved from https://www.betterup.com/blog/triggers

2. Bridges to Recovery. (n.d.). Narcissistic Personality Disorder Relationships. Retrieved from https://www.bridgestorecovery.com/personality-disorders/narcissistic-personality-disorder-relationships/

3. Break the Cycle. (n.d.). Know Your Rights. Retrieved from https://www.breakthecycle.org/know-your-rights/

4. Charlie Health. (n.d.). How Toxic Relationships Affect Your Mental Health. Retrieved from https://www.charliehealth.com/post/how-toxic-relationships-affect-your-mental-health

5. Depth Counseling. (n.d.). How therapy for narcissistic abuse victims can aid healing. Retrieved from https://depthcounseling.org/blog/therapy-for-narcissistic-abuse-victims

6. Domestic Shelters. (n.d.). Ask Amanda: How Can I Regain My Self-Esteem After Abuse? Retrieved from https://www.domesticshelters.org/articles/after-abuse/rebuilding-your-self-esteem-after-abuse

7. Eddins Counseling Group. (n.d.). How To Heal From Emotional Abuse: The Ultimate Guide To ... Retrieved from https://eddinscounseling.com/how-to-heal-from-emotional-abuse/

8. Expressive Art Workshops. (n.d.). 100 Art Therapy Exercises - The Updated and Improved List. Retrieved from https://www.expressiveartworkshops.com/expressive-art-resources/100-art-therapy-exercises/

9. Florida State University Center for Prevention & Early Intervention Policy. (n.d.). LGBT Relationships - Barriers and Complications. Retrieved from https://fsutoolkit.csw.fsu.edu/special-topics/lgbt/lgbt-relationships-barriers-and-complications/

10. Harvard Health Publishing. (n.d.). Having a hobby tied to happiness and well-being. Retrieved from https://www.health.harvard.edu/mind-and-mood/having-a-hobby-tied-to-happiness-and-well-being

11. Healthline. (n.d.). Co-Parenting With a Narcissist: Tips for Making It Work. Retrieved from https://www.healthline.com/health/parenting/co-parenting-with-a-narcissist

12. Healthline. (n.d.). Positive Self-Talk: Benefits and Techniques. Retrieved from https://www.healthline.com/health/positive-self-talk

13. HelpGuide.org. (n.d.). Benefits of Mindfulness. Retrieved from https://www.helpguide.org/harvard/benefits-of-mindfulness.htm

14. HelpGuide.org. (n.d.). Setting Healthy Boundaries in Relationships. Retrieved from https://www.helpguide.org/articles/relationships-communication/setting-healthy-boundaries-in-relationships.htm

15. Her Culture. (2018, December 20). Healing and Moving on After Toxic Friendships. Retrieved from https://www.herculture.org/blog/2018/12/20/healing-and-moving-on-after-toxic-friendships

16. Huffington Post. (2014, February 18). Relationship Success: Balancing Togetherness and Individuality. Retrieved from https://www.huffpost.com/entry/relationship-success-bala_b_4776478

17. LaLa Tigers. (n.d.). Single Parenting after a Toxic Relationship. Retrieved from https://www.lalatigers.com/blog/singe-parenting-after-a-toxic-relationship

18. Leonard, J. (n.d.). Gaslighting: What it is, long-term effects, and what to do. Medical News Today. Retrieved from https://www.medicalnewstoday.com/articles/long-term-effects-of-gaslighting

19. National Center for Biotechnology Information. (2022). Toxic Relationships: The Experiences and Effects. Retrieved from https://www.ncbi.nlm.nih.gov/pmc/articles/PMC9527357/

20. O'Connor, Zoe. "150 Toxic Relationship Quotes To Help You Heal." Paired Magazine. https://www.paired.com/articles/toxic-relationship-quotes

21. Park, M. (2023). How to Set Boundaries With Your Family. TIME. Retrieved from https://time.com/6331383/how-to-set-boundaries-family/

22. Positive Psychology. (n.d.). 15 Values Worksheets to Enrich Clients' Lives (+ Inventory). Retrieved from https://positivepsychology.com/values-worksheets/

23. Positive Psychology. (n.d.). 7 Ways to Improve Communication in Relationships. Retrieved from https://positivepsychology.com/communication-in-relationships/

24. Positive Psychology. (n.d.). Conflict Resolution in Relationships & Couples: 5 Strategies. Retrieved from https://positivepsychology.com/conflict-resolution-relationships/

25. Psychology Today. (2022, July). 6 Steps Toward Recovery From a Toxic Relationship. Retrieved from https://www.psychologytoday.com/us/blog/invisible-bruises/202207/6-steps-toward-recovery-toxic-relationship

26. Scary Mommy. (n.d.). You Can't Co-Parent With A Toxic Ex, But You Can Do This ... Retrieved from https://www.scarymommy.com/cant-co-parenting-with-a-toxic-ex

27. Sources of Insight. (n.d.). How To Build Vulnerability-Based Trust on Your

Team. Retrieved from https://sourcesofinsight.com/building-trust-on-your-teams/

28. study.com. (n.d.). Emotional Bullying Definition, Effects & Examples - Lesson. Retrieved from https://study.com/academy/lesson/emotional-bullying-definition-facts-examples.html

29. Tschosik, E. (n.d.). How to Leave an Abusive Relationship Safely. Verywell Mind. Retrieved from https://www.verywellmind.com/making-a-safety-plan-to-escape-abusive-relationship-5069959

30. Verywell Mind. (n.d.). How to Find a Narcissistic Abuse Support Group. Retrieved from https://www.verywellmind.com/how-to-find-a-narcissistic-abuse-support-group-5271477

31. Weaver, S. (2023, August 12). The harsh impact of gaslighting in romantic relationships. Deseret News. Retrieved from https://www.deseret.com/2023/8/12/23794050/gaslighting-in-romantic-relationships-abuse/

32. Zurbuch, J. (n.d.). Rebuilding Your Finances After Financial Abuse. Bankrate. Retrieved from https://www.bankrate.com/personal-finance/rebuild-finances-after-financial-abuse/

Bonus
12 STEPS TO FREEDOM

Sometimes the hardest part isn't letting go but rather learning to start over.

Nicole Sobon

1. Acknowledgment

Step: Admit to yourself that the relationship is toxic and that it's affecting your well-being. Reflection: What were the key moments that made you realize the relationship is toxic?

2. Seek Support

Step: Reach out to friends, family, or a therapist who can provide emotional support and guidance. Reflection: Who in your life makes you feel supported and understood?

3. Document Your Feelings

Step: Keep a journal of how you feel in and about the relationship to track your emotional state over time. Reflection: How do your entries change over time? What patterns do you notice?

4. Set Boundaries

Step: Begin setting clear boundaries with the other person about what is no longer acceptable to you. Reflection: How does setting these boundaries make you feel? Empowered? Guilty? Relieved?

5. Create an Exit Plan

Step: Plan how you will separate from the person, including logistical details like finances, living arrangements, and communication. Reflection: What are your biggest fears about leaving, and how can you address them?

6. Build Independence

Step: Focus on personal growth and self-sufficiency. Engage in activities that build your self-esteem and independence. Reflection: What new activities or old passions have you rediscovered that make you feel good about yourself?

7. Communicate Clearly

Step: Have a direct conversation with the person about your decision to end the relationship. Reflection: How did preparing for this conversation make you feel? What reactions did you anticipate?

8. Act

Step: Execute your exit plan. This may involve moving out, separating accounts, and other necessary steps. Reflection: How did it feel to take these actions? Were there unexpected challenges or reliefs?

9. Seek Legal Advice

Step: If necessary, consult with a legal professional to handle any legalities like divorce, custody, or restraining orders. Reflection: What have you learned about your rights and legal protections through this process?

10. Limit Contact

Step: Minimize or eliminate contact with the person, depending on your specific circumstances. Reflection: How has reducing contact affected your emotional and mental health?

11. Heal and Reflect

Step: Give yourself time to heal. Engage in therapy or healing practices like meditation, exercise, or hobbies. Reflection: What healing practices have been most effective for you? How do you feel different now than before you started?

12. Plan for the Future

Step: Begin to plan your life post-relationship. Set goals for yourself and imagine your future without the toxic relationship. Reflection: What are you most looking forward to in your future? How do you envision yourself growing from this experience?